SAME GAME
NEW RULES

23 TIMELESS PRINCIPLES FOR SELLING AND NEGOTIATING

Join us at our website for

more insight and developmental work.

www.samegamenewrules.com

SAME GAME
NEW RULES

23 TIMELESS PRINCIPLES
FOR SELLING AND NEGOTIATING

BILL CASKEY

WINPOINTE PUBLISHING

CARMEL, INDIANA

Winpointe Publishing
4971 Waterside Circle
Carmel, IN 46033

Copyright © 2006 William B. Caskey

ISBN 0-9758510-3-9

Editorial: Bill Caskey
Editing: Amy Balcius
Text Design: Desktop Miracles
Cover Design: Rob Larsen

Printed in the USA on acid-free paper

10 9 8 7 6 5 4 3 2 1

ACKNOWLEDGMENTS

Anyone in the personal development business knows this truth: our clients are our trainers. Sure, we can think up all the greatest theories and read like crazy until we formulate axioms. But until it passes the client test and the market test, it's worthless. So I'm grateful to every client we've ever had pass through the doors. You have helped us take this material and apply it to the real world in a way we could never have done alone. For that, I'm personally grateful. We have the best clients on the planet.

Along with that, no book is ever completed without the support of the family and extended family of the author. Jane, Kelly, Kara, Bill, Norine, Don, Sally—you all gave me support throughout this project. I'm very grateful.

TABLE OF CONTENTS

The Insights

FOREWORD

When Bill asked me to write the foreword, I must admit, I became very uncomfortable. Why would I want to put my success with these principles out there for everyone to see? What if my competitors read this and became familiar with the thought process we were using to take market share? Couldn't that affect us negatively? Wouldn't it be kind of like allowing your competition to see a copy of your play-book?

I came to my senses quickly when I realized two things. First, my company has a five-year head start in practicing these principles of achievement. So even if my competitors began today, I suspect we'd be a few yards ahead of them. I must tell you—on the journey we've lost some who weren't able to change. But those left are high producers and much of the reason for that is within these pages.

Secondly, I truly believe every market is abundant. A rising tide lifts all boats. If we can all get better at the game of business, then we'll all be stronger.

I met Bill in June of 1996. I had just joined Midwest Bankers and began his workshops. It was part of the personal development that Midwest Bankers provides its people. I had never been through formal sales training and was excited by the concept. As a self-professed personal development junkie, having an actual class to attend on how to improve my income was nirvana.

Actually, this class was very similar to the finance training I received in college. Finance is a branch of applied micro-economics—a very fertile and conceptual branch with lots of real world applications. So there I was in the midst of a fertile, conceptual learning environment with an unlimited number of real world applications.

As I moved through his training and adopted the insights you will see here, there were only two words to describe them—simple and elegant. They are simple because it is said that you get what you ask for in life and in business, so you'd better be precise in your request. If you aren't living the life you want, then look inside yourself and determine what you asked for. Are you a million-dollar salesperson or are you a $50,000 salesperson? Whichever you think, you become. This is the essence of the inner game.

These rules of thought are elegant because they teach you how to *attract* income rather than teach you how to *sell*. No more putting heavy pressure on people to do business with you. It doesn't work now and it never has, but until now we haven't had a selling philosophy to substitute for the antiquated selling tactics that 90% of the market uses.

If you're a salesperson today and are resistant to changing your approach, then put this book down. It will be a dramatic change from what most people have been exposed to and will be a challenge for you to implement. Most people will fall into this category, which is why 35.1% of America's wealth is owned by 1% of American households.

Conversely, if you are in sales and thrive on improving yourself and are consciously looking for new ways and better thoughts, then read this book and begin to implement these principles immediately. As CEO, I get called on by a lot of supposed top performers and it's apparent that few have adopted these unconventional, yet profoundly effective techniques. By doing so, you will conclude, like I have, that it's not just solving the problem that allows you to get the business, but it's how you approach people.

If you are a CEO or manager and are considering passing this out to your team, read it first and buy in to the concepts.

Make sure you're a believer. Then insist that the sales force reads the material and discusses each chapter at a sales meeting. The 20% of the team that produces 80% of the results will probably implement the concepts. The newer people not yet on the sales radar screen may surprise you. This could be just what they need to get started. But don't expect everyone to adopt these rules. Some just won't have the capacity—and that's OK.

Caskey's elegant and simple approach to dealing with the pesky humans in business is both refreshing and transforming. The beautiful part of the entire philosophy is that most people won't be able to handle the changes in thought required to implement the approach. Why is that beautiful? As CEO of a company that buys into it, the people that won't change make our lives easier. The companies of the future will be nimble and very adaptive. Those who have sales teams that resist changing their thoughts will end up at our competition. And yours, too. Just hope your competitor doesn't buy this book.

DAVID CATALANO
CEO, MIDWEST BANKERS
INDIANAPOLIS, FALL 2000
dcatalano@midwestbankers.com

PREFACE

It was late fall of 1995 and I was in Memphis for a two-day program. It was a group of long-distance telephone salespeople. I had been delivering on-going training programs for sales groups for many years and this group, in comparison to the rest, was **very average**. As usual, it took us the first few hours of the session to get comfortable with each other. And there was the normal resistance to my concepts.

The next few hours of discussion were not so average.

As you could probably guess, these people faced a ton of competition. Long-distance telephone salespeople in the mid 90's were barraging business owners with the latest and greatest rate plans. One of the people in the group was told by a prospect that over thirty long-distance companies had contacted him in the last thirty days. So as you can imagine (and perhaps your business is similar), they had a huge "differentiation" problem. When they called and did their traditional pitch and sounded like everybody else, they got treated like everybody else—rejected or commoditized. This is where the discussion got interesting.

The group arrived that morning expecting to hear the same thing the last 10 trainers told them. By now, you know the commands—call higher, probe deeper, close harder. After all, that's what every other sales trainer on the planet tells you. I decided to take a risk that day and talk about something they hadn't heard. The problem for these salespeople was not that they didn't know what to say. It was that they didn't know how to think. They had skills training—plenty of it. Their training had been given by one of the largest development companies in the land. They had attended the one and two sem-inars to pump them full of life force and vigor. They had the books and tapes from Amer-ica's finest motivators; but it was all useless, because no one had taught them the most important ingredient—the glue which holds it all together—**how to think**. They had the right moves, but not the right thoughts.

> No man is a good physician
> who has never been sick.
>
> *ARAB PROVERB*

This group was thinking "scarcity"

As it turned out, this group was thinking from a vola-tile position—that of scarcity. High competition and price pressure had created demons in the brains of these reps. The outcome was this: they were approaching the market thinking and acting like beggars. They ended up getting so emotionally attached to every deal that they were actually repelling their prospects with their neediness. So we began talking about what has come to be known as the Inner Game Concept.

I finally said, "Look, let's get real—let me remind you of the facts you've forgotten—you don't need any piece of business to be OK in life. Unemployment is 4.5% in Memphis—if you can't sell long-distance, you can find something else to do. There are 10,000 prospects that need what you have and if someone is not open to even discussing it, hang up and move on. You need to reject these prospects before they reject you." I continued, "You're going to wake up tomorrow morning OK psycho-logically whether you make another sale or not. In the next 40 years if you don't make another sale, you're going to be OK. God is not going to send a lightning bolt to your back-side just because you didn't make your quota for the month. So get rid of your fear." When I was finished, I sensed something magical had happened. Their stares changed. Their minds raced. Their looks became inquisitive.

As I left the training room, a man approached me. He had sat in the back both days, "Can I have a few minutes of your time?" I agreed and he began to talk. He said, "You know what you're teaching don't you?"

"Well, I thought I did, but I'm curious—what did you learn?"

He said, "What you're really teaching is a form of business spirituality that is missing in today's corporate life."

"Okay," I said. "Can you elaborate?"

He continued, "Do you know what could happen to my income and the sales of all our people if we could come to grips with the fact that everything is going to be OK if we don't sell anything tomorrow?"

I said, "That's exactly my point."

"I know it is, but what you've done is you've taken the fear out of selling. If I'm ever worried about my family not eating or my not making quota or getting fired or getting shamed in front of my peers—and there is a fear that accompanies those feelings—I will pass it on to my prospect when I'm on the phone or in front of them."

> Learning is not attained by chance. It must be sought for with ardor and attended to with diligence.
>
> ABIGAIL ADAMS

He said, "It means the one thing I am afraid of is the very thing I am attracting to me. Rejection. It also means if I can get past that hurdle, I'll be able to take risks from now on and never be scared. That's what is "spiritual" about it. You've made all of us think how business, selling and life all interconnect. Thank you."

As I left the room that day I had a funny feeling in my heart. I actually felt like my life had changed with that conversation. I don't know who that man was and he probably doesn't remember me. But in five short minutes he taught me more than I'm sure I taught him in the entire sixteen hours of training. This philosophy does more than help you sell— it helps you reframe the way business and life and the systems governing both are blended to optimize your future. It forces you to question your deepest thoughts about self, role and marketplace. It propels you to think new, contemporary thoughts about how you achieve. The new rules are upon us.

> As a general rule, the most successful man in life is the man who has the best information.
>
> BENJAMIN DISRAELI

I'd like to hear from you personally

Incidentally, work like this is never complete. I tell people in our programs that personal development is not about an agenda. It's a matter of continuous improvement. Thus, I'm very interested in your thoughts on your journey as you implement these strategies of thought. Won't you please e-mail me at author@samegamenewrules.com and share with me your results—successes and failures? The internet is a wonderful tool to build direct communication between author and reader and I'd like to use it for that.

INTRODUCTION

If God does not exist and you believe in him, then little harm is done. But if God does exist and you don't believe in him, great harm is done.

Blaise Pascal
16th-Century Mathematician

You may read this book cover to cover. You may write to me, e-mail me, come to our programs and find at the end, that these insights won't help you reach the kinds of sales level and confidence that you had hoped. You may find they do not help you in solving the problems which most sellers and marketers have. If that occurs, then there is no harm done—a little time, a little money, and a little pride. Old Thinking is still available to you. You can always go back.

But if there exists in these pages and in our observations a quantum change in your perspective that will profoundly influence your thought process, your approach to your business and your income, then it would be a great mistake to ignore it. We can only hope that we've presented these thought changes in a way that you can absorb. Changing your perspective slightly affects your results profoundly.

Our intention was to compile and fuse several philosophies of business, life, selling and high achievement. The study for this led us to many philosophies, teachers and their literary works. You have heard the names before—Christ, Descartes, James, Allen, Emerson, Coleridge, Nietzsche, Schopenhauer. You have also heard of their contemporary counterparts like Fromm, Harris, Berne, Leaman, Freud, Covey, Robbins, Bradshaw and Dyer. Through that study, I thought I would get all I would need to assemble the secrets of success in sales achievement. But I was wrong. My missing link was you.

> A good archer is known not by his arrows, but by his aim.
>
> ENGLISH PROVERB

You, or people like you, were my teachers. The Sams, Curts, Karens, Rogers, Jeffs and Ritas. They are obscure on the national scene, but instrumental in helping me assemble a condensed set of insights that we hope will help millions. Theory is worthless until there is a live application to test it on.

As Dale Carnegie once said:

> *The ideas I stand for are not mine. I borrowed them from Socrates, I swiped them from Chesterfield, I stole them from Jesus, and I put them in a book. If you don't like their rules, whose would you use?*

These "new rules of thought" were created with the intent to help salespeople and marketers think differently.

R U L E

If you want to change your results, you must change your actions. And if you hope to change your actions over a sustained period of time, you must change your thoughts.

If I can help you change your thoughts, the new actions happen quickly and effortlessly. No more 400-page sales training manuals. No more long, boring weekly training

2

meetings back at home office. No more learning how to sell the hard way. Instead, these insights, if practiced, will lead you to a new thought form about how to communicate the enormous personal value you have in your business.

Who Should Read This Book?

This book is for people in the profession of sales and marketing who are searching for an easier, softer, more effective way to build their income. Each day in the U.S. alone, more than 25 million people are responsible in some way for their company's revenue, or their client's satisfaction. These are the salespeople, account developers, accountants, attorneys, engineers, managers, project heads, doctors and thousands of other professionals. Each day, these people have conversations with their prospects and clients about their businesses. It's also for people in one or more of these categories.

'Tis skill not strength which governs a ship.

THOMAS FULLER
Gnomologia

- Those who have seen the one-day seminars, have bought the books, have listened to the tapes of the greatest speakers in the world—and yet, are still looking for the one philosophy or approach that fits their style.
- People who want their selling method to support their personal strength, yet not compromise their dignity or that of their prospects.
- Those companies having salespeople who are, in large part, responsible for the success and future of their companies.

The book is for those who want to help manage themselves and their sales process by using a systematic and contemporary method. Quite simply it is for those pioneers who dare to be different.

Why I Wrote This Book

I wrote this book for several reasons, all of which may not apply to you.

1. THE WEAK TACTICS USED BY MOST AMERICAN SALES FORCES ARE DISAPPOINTING.

I believe professional selling is a noble profession—as noble as it gets—yet the training we are giving today's salespeople belittles the salesperson and sacrifices his dignity in the sales process. If you want to understand what I am talking about, do this: when a salesperson solicits you over the next two weeks, just sit back and let them sell. Listen intently to how they communicate with you. Note in your head how you feel. Pay careful attention to the tactics they use to get you bought into what they are selling. Ask yourself if they're out for you—or themselves. And then ask yourself this: "Is that the way I sound when I'm pursuing new business?"

> The only real voyage of discovery consists not of seeking new landscapes but in having new eyes.
>
> *MARCEL PROUST*

The true role of the sales professional today is to facilitate the prospect's sharing of information with you that he wouldn't ordinarily share. And to do it in a way that is helping him do three things:

- One—understand his real problem or opportunity.
- Two—understand the value you bring in helping him solve those problems.
- Three—get his problem solved.

The conventional approach that most salespeople take to the market actually puts the prospect in control. The old strategies are based on nothing more than manipulation and coercion. What's worse—they stopped working long ago. On those occasions when they do work, you settle for the $40,000 deal and are blind to the $400,000 deal slightly beneath the surface. The sad part is, you seldom know what happened. If you're OK with that, then continue on in the same vein, calling on way too many prospects, making way too many proposals, getting just enough business to pay your bills. It's been my experience that sales and marketing people who refuse to look at these strategies and tactics will consistently underachieve.

> He who cannot change the very fabric of his thought will never be able to change reality.
>
> ANWAR EL-SADAT

To sum up—get out of the carnage of the current paradigm and move into a new thinking strategy about your personal achievement in this ancient game of selling.

2. IT FRUSTRATES ME TO SEE COMPANIES WITH EXCELLENT PRODUCTS AND SERVICES AND EXCELLENT SUPPORT AND DELIVERY MECHANISMS, WHOSE SALES STAFFS ARE UNTRAINED TO COMMUNICATE THAT VALUE.

So they go to a strategic consultant who leaves after several years and hundreds of thousands (or millions) of dollars. The company has nothing more than a useless PowerPoint "strategic plan" that takes a Harvard Ph.D. to decipher.

The fact is, and always was, that the selling company had absolutely no method to translate their core value to prospects and clients. Management erroneously figured that "if we give the salespeople great compensation plans, laptop computers, e-mail addresses and six-color brochures, they could sell better." Sorry to disappoint you, but they were given the wrong things. They were given toys, not skills in how to translate value.

How do you know when you're not communicating your value well? Simple. The following things happen:

- You're held hostage by large clients.
- You have long selling cycles that wear you out.
- You never get the truth from the prospect.
- You never feel like you have an honest relationship with your potential prospect.
- You get beaten down on price.
- You can't even get in the front door.
- You feel undignified in the selling process.
- You feel like a beggar.

Do any of these sound familiar?

3. CHANGING PEOPLE'S THINKING HAS PROFOUND EFFECTS ON THEIR RESULTS AND INCOME.

I've been coaching and working with thousands of people in the last 18 years. I have given over 3000 workshops to virtually every type of industry and group, including salespeople, executive teams, and project managers. It never fails after a full-day program, I meet people who tell me, "This will change how I sell and approach people," or "This makes so much sense, I can't believe I never thought of it," or, "This method will make me tons of money."

One example of a major thought change is "detachment." It is really a quite simple and elegant philosophy. But because it hasn't been taught to America's sales forces, those sales forces are operating at a less than optimal level. In this case, one small change in thought about "detaching from deals" will yield huge results in revenue.

4. Philosophy Helps You Excel.

I believe in philosophy. I think we all need better and clearer philosophies on achievement, education, wealth creation, selling, marketing, communication, child rearing, etc. We tend to be a society that flip-flops around according to the latest trend or business book. I want you to have a philosophy about prospecting, about your time, about your personal and mental strength, about your creative potential and your expression of that potential. I don't want you to just know HOW to do it; I think it is important first to know WHY.

If you have a philosophy that you truly live by, the techniques and tactics will come naturally, quickly and easily. My role is to share a philosophy that we feel affords you the best recipe for personal growth. From that, you will establish your own rules and philosophy. Consequently, in Appendix B, on page 181 at the end of the book, I have left space for you to write those rules. The new rules should be yours, not mine. I'm here to give you rules around which you can create new thoughts for achievement. Your job is to make them personal.

> It is impossible to endure the *how*, until one first understands the *why*.
>
> FRIEDRICH NIETZSCHE

5. When the Message Is Good, Share It With the Masses.

The truth is, I'm just one guy. I can't be everywhere, but I can document these strategies and belief changes. I have seen lives turn around with these insights. I've personally witnessed transformations in peoples' careers once they accepted and adopted these new rules of thought. I've seen multi-millionaires created after a short time of using these thinking strategies. Thus, if these insights can help even a few people create more personal income and return credibility and dignity to what sometimes can be a tough profession, then I'll be satisfied. There are hundreds of excellent books on topics like strategic territory planning, time management, goal setting and effective presentations. Many of these we've listed in the "recommended reading" section in the appendix. We, however, prefer to focus on the deeper topic—*the thinking behind sales achievement.*

About the Insights

How to Get the Most from This Book

My goal throughout this book is to have a personal conversation with you—yet not be preachy. And even though I don't know you personally, in my 18 years of coaching I've most likely helped similar people develop. Consequently, I know that you and I may have to get together more than once. You may read this book once now—then again in a month—and receive two very different messages. So my first plea is for you to read this book at least twice.

Second, I've intentionally kept this book small so you can carry it along with you. Prior to every call or client meeting, thumb through the book and spend a minute on an insight. Don't try to pick out the perfect insight—just read one. After thirty to forty repetitions of this, you will see dramatic change in how you view and execute your sales process.

Third, you will notice that some insights are a page or less and some are longer. Those longer insights contain more background and stories to help you grasp their meaning. Some might argue that the longer the insight, the more important it is. You'll have to judge the truth in that yourself.

Lastly, I've left space at the end for you to write your own philosophy book. Create your own playbook on how you'll approach business from here on out. I've even given you a sample from someone who has attended our workshops and completed the exercises.

The Fundamental Philosophies

Just as I am asking you to build your own philosophy from our input, it is important that I let you in on some of our overriding philosophies of selling, buying and business. These beliefs and assumptions have come after thousands of hours of observation. Here they are in no particular order:

ALL SELLING IS PERSONAL

If you are in the business of communicating the value of your company to another person from the prospect or client company, then you know what I mean when I say selling is personal. Yes, your firm has value. Yes, you make the best widget in the land. And yes, your pricing is competitive. But at the bell, it's you and the prospect. And your ability to transfer the value that you have—to a form he understands and is willing to pay for—is a very personal matter. It's also personal because your thoughts will get in the way. Your prior beliefs will sabotage you. The fear that you have will appear at just the wrong time and screw you up, unless you have a strong process of thought and action.

> A moment's insight
> is sometimes worth
> a life's experience.
>
> OLIVER WENDEL HOLMES

ALL PROBLEMS HAVE AN INNER ORIGIN

In business there is profound wealth to be earned by solving problems. Anyone who wimps away from talking about problems is crazy—for that's where all of the extra profit is. But did you ever think that all problems in business start in someone's head—someone's inner game? It's true. Take the most common problem you have in the sales process and I'll wager with you that it is, in part, a "head problem." Here's an example: "Not enough time in the day" is one of the most common answers to the question, "What's the biggest thing you struggle with in sales?" But look deeper and you'll find it is an inner problem. After further questioning with the client, I always find that it isn't a "not enough time" problem. It is a "my-ego-is-too-attached-to-delegate-problem," which has to do with the inner game.

To not even speak of the thoughts which exist in the minds of today's seller is absurd. As you read these insights, be prepared to deal with the real problem—how you think. That is the prime issue of the "Inner Game." You will hear us talk about the "Inner Game" in these pages. It is the "head" part of sales. It is the mental strategy that you bring with you to your business. It is the fear or conviction that underlies your assumptions about life. It is the abundance or scarcity attitude you have of the Universe. It is the head game you play with yourself about personal achievement. A good, strong Inner Game means you will be able to do the following:

> Money makes a good servant
> but a terrible master.
>
> *FRENCH PROVERB*

Learn, grow, expand, earn more, see opportunity, be unafraid of outcomes, be a good communicator, have a good self-image, be detached, have fun, see abundance, be a good listener.

A weak inner game will result in the following:

Fear, constriction, closed-mindedness, denial, attachment to what people think of you, fear of taking risks, restriction, worry, too much talking.

WE USE ONLY A FRACTION OF OUR TRUE POTENTIAL

I know, I know. How many times have you heard this one? Enough to make you believe it? I hope so, because it's true. Most brain researchers will tell you that we use five to seven percent of our brain capacity, which is another way of saying we use five to seven percent of our potential. It's our philosophy that to achieve at a different level, you must use your brain more. And when you make marginal improvements in brain activity, you get quantum changes in results.

> Insight doesn't happen often on the click of the moments . . . but comes in its own time and from nowhere but within.
>
> EUDORA WELTY
> *One Place, One Time*

Consequently, we will give you some brain food in these insights which you may not agree with up front. But as you mull them over, read them a few times and bring them up at a sales or staff meeting, you'll begin to see they're sound.

THE WORLD IS ABUNDANT REGARDLESS OF THE CONDITION OF THE ECONOMY

I believe that each of us has an infinite power available to us. It's there for the asking. It's there when you have faith in the market's ability and desire to provide you with anything you want. The market is abundant because your mind is abundant. Your creativity is abundant. Your thoughts are infinite. So use them to create wealth for yourself and your company.

LEARNING IS PROFITABLE, ONGOING AND INCREMENTAL

I don't believe high achievers get there overnight. There are always a few overnight sensations, but their foundations are usually built on shaky ground. Sound improvement takes place over time and requires intense commitment—to self, to growth and to company. Those who set out wanting to have it all, yet are not willing to change their thoughts to get there are in for a long winter. Learning is incremental because we don't learn in

> Be careful of your own thoughts; they may become words at any minute.
>
> IARA GASSEN

big doses—but in small ones. That's why I prefer you read this book a couple of times through—five minutes at a time—so that you allow your thoughts to change from the previous exposure. As you do that, you will see incremental change happen.

The Wrap

The basic fundamental is this: If you continue to look at selling as an art form, you will under-achieve because you will ignore the basic laws of personal growth. Instead, look at selling like you would look at driving a car, running a business, managing a team, or playing a sport. Look at selling for what it is: A ROLE. When you look at selling that way, you will be more able to improve your skills in that role.

When we attempt to improve our success/performance in any role, we know we must undertake a "role-improvement strategy." That strategy consists of two faces: the inner game and the outer game. In other words, there is the mental version and the physical version of the role. And to work only on one of those is self-limiting.

An Example

It's the NBA Championship final game—game seven. A player steps to the line with :01 on the clock and down by one point. He has two free throws. If he hits both, they win the world championship. If he misses both, they lose. Pretty simple, right? Let's also suppose that this player hit 89% of his free throws over the course of the season. Based on these facts, tell me what you think the odds are that he will hit both shots.

Before you answer that, let me ask you this: Is there more going on here than shooting free throws? Of course, you say. But wait a minute. He's still 15 feet from the basket. He still has ten seconds to shoot. The basket is still ten feet high. He still has his same technique to summon. The crowd noise is still the same. So, why do you think it's different?

If he has these same two shots in practice, he probably will hit 95% of them, but when the pressure increases, everything changes. If he puts too much pressure on himself, what do you suppose will happen to his technique? If he shoulders the weight of his team, his city, and his division, feeling all of that pressure, do you think he'll be calm at the line? Probably not. The Inner Game—the mental game—of the player figures into his performance.

This is not unlike your inner game when you get into a high-pressure situation. Maybe you're in front of the CEO when you're used to calling on the plant manager. Maybe you're in front of a board of directors when you're used to calling on individuals. Maybe you're calling on a company that could generate ten times the business that most of your clients do. Maybe you're calling on a company where you absolutely NEED the business. Whatever the scenario, your inner game figures strongly in the outcome. And no where is the inner game so important as in the little word: *focus*.

In your role performance, your focus must be disciplined. Your focus should always deal with your prospect, rather than yourself. Your focus will do more to profoundly increase your income than any other strategy you have. If you can consciously focus on creating the environment where your prospect reveals the truth to you about his or her pain, problems, vision or needs, it doesn't matter if you're calling on Bill Gates or Billy Bob Gatlin. **By you disciplining your focus, you are not at all concerned about what a person thinks of you.** You aren't concerned with whether you're going to get this deal or not (worrying about that is the curse of death in professional selling). You aren't worried at all about whether your name will sit atop the contest chart at the end of the quarter. You aren't worried about whether you talk his language or ask the right questions. Your focus is on him and his worries, concerns and struggles.

And when you can do that, the inner game becomes strong, clear and powerful. You will have successfully detoured around the ego and gone right to the spirit, which is where you're the most powerful.

You will approach every new prospect or situation from a place of stewardship—helping people reveal to you their problems—to determine if you can help them. You will become an authentic person rather than some mask-wearing annoying salesperson who cares only about himself and his quota. You will become an abundant being in the marketplace with little or no fear. Why? You know that there is enough pain out there to keep you busy and make you wealthy.

You will have awakened abundance within yourself and the marketplace by re-focusing on their problems, their pain, and their consequences, and kept your pain and ego out of the mix. This is what these insights are about: your achievement in the role of selling.

TRENDS SHAPING SELLING

Markets Are Ultra-Competitive

There are few real differential advantages today. Cycle times between an introduction of an innovative product and the time when another company copies it are measured in weeks, not years. The internet propels this even faster. Because of this, companies are hungry for any advantage they can find. That advantage rests in the sales process through which companies take their buyers. It isn't about features and benefits all of the time. THERE IS PROFOUND ADVANTAGE IN A GOOD PROCESS. If you aren't constantly looking at the process through which you take your clients on the way to the purchase, someone else is sneaking up on you and will grab market share. Features and benefits are of little use in separating your product from others. If you believe you bring value, then what is your system of translating that value in a way that your prospect understands and is willing to pay for?

Client Decision-Making Is More Complex

Today, it's harder to get to the decision-makers. There must be meticulous processes in place to manage the sales cycle when you can't get to everyone within the prospect company. Committees crop up within companies—everyone is talking about empowerment but few are walking the walk.

If you're the seller, the question becomes, "How do I advance the sales process with ten decision makers, instead of one?" Plus, when you have 10 decision-makers, it becomes harder to know everyone's compelling issue. It's hard enough to get one person to tell you the truth, but trying to get ten people to level with you, when they probably aren't telling each other the truth, is beyond comprehension. If you don't have the mental toughness to get to the compelling reason for each person in the group, you will be trying to put together a puzzle without all of the pieces.

That is why the sales skill of the next millennium is "orchestration." How you move through the prospect/client company is critical. If you expect your contact or champion to do it for you, you may be expecting too much.

Corporate Weave

There is so much cross-over or weave between companies and industries that it becomes confusing. And if you are one of those people who have multiple product lines, you must, MUST figure out a way to have a high-level conversation with your potential client, or you will be dropped right back into the price/features game, which you'll rarely win.

The phone people are in networking. The cable people are in phone systems. The insurance people are in banking. The bankers are in mortgages and insurance. And everyone builds websites. On and on it goes. And because of that "weave," the decision-making processes in the business-to-business areas are becoming longer and more complex. If the salesperson or marketer doesn't know how to take a person from suspect to prospect to client stage effectively, without pushing and pressuring, they will be held hostage to their prospect's system, which seldom has the best interest of the salesperson in mind.

So, as a sales professional, you must be meticulous at laying out what you do, how you do it, and some of your philosophies behind your action—quickly and clearly. If there is any confusion in the prospect's mind, they won't wait around for you to improve your communication skills. They'll find someone else to buy from.

Labor Pool

Companies want to keep and train their best salespeople because the labor pool is small. Firing and recruiting is expensive so companies are looking for alternative ways to grow revenues and train salespeople.

They want to maximize the leverage they get for the investment they make in the salesperson. They hire a salesperson for $75,000, put him in a car and give him an expense account and the perks, and he is up to $100,000 very quickly. **The best place you can build market value in a company is in the sales process.** If you have 20 sales-people bringing in $2M each, and through training you can increase that by 50% (which shouldn't be a problem as long as the company can deliver), you have just increased your company's market value by $10M. You can go out and buy other companies or spend $1M in marketing, but the value is sitting right in front of you . . . in your sales force.

Companies want to optimize that investment as soon as they can. Today's contemporary-thinking company can't devote two years to a salesperson to develop their business. If a salesperson can't be advancing deals in 60 days, then their process is wrong. Developing the sales force will fix that problem. Companies today don't want people who have proven they can act, they want people who have proven they can think.

If You're a Sales Professional

You are being hit with higher quotas, more responsibilities (more planning, project management, tracking of prospects and clients etc.) and non-selling activities. That all means that when you're in front of your prospect, you have to be extra effective. Marketing departments aren't providing the leads they should, so it's left up to the sales team to generate their own leads. You must be part marketer, part relationship developer, part closer, and part CEO. You have your hands full with customers who want more for less and company people who still don't see the value you bring.

You have it extra tough. We'll help.

If You're an Owner

You are looking to get paid more for the value that you've created in your business. Yes, you can continue to put systems in place that deliver more value for your clients and customers, but you also must have a *system which helps your people translate* the value you've already built. If you have 100 units of value but your sales team is only able to translate 70% of that, then you will see selling cycles lengthen, discounting continue, and you will experience a general under-utilization of your sales asset—your sales force. The trends we've stated above are the conditions of the marketplace under which you must work.

Consequently, everything in this book is written with the intent of helping you and your people develop a strategy for translating or communicating your value in a manner that helps you get paid for that value in the marketplace.

THE FUNDAMENTAL SHIFT

There are great books that depict the fundamental shift occurring in American Business today. Jim Collins, in his book *Good to Great*, talks about the fundamental shift in looking at your organization. Steve Walker, in *Stakeholder Power*, talks about the fundamental shift of how we see customer loyalty. And Geoffrey Moore, *Beyond The Chasm*, talks about the fundamental shift in business models needed to grow a business. While I've read those books and believe they are of great value, I've yet to see a book addressing the fundamental shift required in the business-to-business sales world.

As I travel to sales training meetings, I always begin the day by asking 'what are some of the problems you're having in the sales process?' Invariably, I find these problems are the same regardless of what city I was in—or what industry I was in.

Actually, it wasn't until I was asked by a client to 'boil your whole philosophy down to three core principles' that I discovered what a miserable job I was doing in helping people change their thinking. I was teaching people how to go out and do different things—but I was never teaching them **how to think differently**—how to make a shift in thought that resulted in a shift in results.

The sales problems I hear from senior managers come about because of lousy thought. If you've heard yourself (or your people) saying these things, then it may be time for a shift.

- "My customer just doesn't get our value."
- "We're having to discount too much to get the business."

- "We need to make the sales process more efficient."
- "We had a better proposal—how did our competitor get it?"
- "I'm getting tired of rejection."
- "I don't have enough deals in my sales funnel."
- Or, "How do I handle it when my prospect says 'your price is too high'?"

If you've said those things, your thinking may be old and worn out. You need a radically new way to think about selling that requires a **fundamental shift** in philosophy. Warning: This new mode of thinking will obsolete the current sales tactics (they haven't changed for generations so maybe that's not a problem) that you might currently be using.

Here's my belief: **All sales problems can be solved by a shift in sales philosophy.** And that's what we'll talk about in this book.

So why the required shift?

1. **Globalization:** You are competing today not only with the vendor across town but with a vendor or solution that can come from anywhere in the world. You don't just have to be 'as good as' the competitor in the same market. You have to be 'as good or better than' the best in the world—maybe not at delivering value—but you have to be better than the rest at **expressing** your value.

2. **Commoditization:** People will pay more for your value but only if **you** understand it and are effective at communicating it. In my consulting practice I work with organizations who believe they bring a different value to the table but upon closer inspection it's all nauseatingly the same. You can go to rah-rah motivational meanings all you want but if your offer

looks exactly the same as everyone else's you won't get far in the market and you'll end up competing on price, where no one wins. Your effort should be in the **understanding and expression** of your value.

3. **Relevance:** People will pay for your value if it's relevant to them—to the extent that it either (a) **solves a problem** or (b) **exploits an opportunity.** Your customer has neither the time nor the expertise to figure out if your solution solves a problem or exploits a possibility. A value proposition (I despise that term) that doesn't do one or both of those things is not really valuable to the customer. What's more, your value must speak to the customer in *their* language or you'll get NO credit for it.

4. **Skepticism:** You won't get to the customer's problems or opportunities if you don't make it safe for him to reveal them. The old sales process of **convince, persuade and defend** closes the communication channel rather than opens it. It makes them skeptical about anything you say. Stop looking at it as: "how do I get my customer to understand my value?" Start looking at it as, "How can I create the environment where he can reveal his problems so I can help him understand the value I provide?"

The Fundamental Shift You Must Make In Selling

In our training practice we have worked with hundreds of companies in an array of industries: enterprise software, distribution, logistics, accounting, dentistry, capital equipment, banking and financial, etc. Since 1989, we've written hundreds of hours of curriculum that helps companies solve sales problems.

But it wasn't until a year ago that I realized we made a dramatic error in how we presented that material. After a six-month engagement, one of our clients said, "Bill, I love your curriculum, but can't you give us two or three key principles that you could boil it down to so that everything fits underneath?"

Consequently, I devised three fundamental shifts in our thinking that will influence how we act in the market— and also impact the results we get. And this entire book supports one or more of these fundamental shifts.

1. **From Scarcity To Abundance. (How We See the Market.)** It never fails to amaze me at the scarcity complex that we have for our future. When we look at our market, most of us don't see abundance. We see constriction, lack and scarcity. We, wrongly, look at our pipeline of new business and use that as a metric for market abundance. **How you see the world influences how you approach the world.** That's why the Number One shift must be a shift to **seeing the world as a place of abundance.** When you see abundance rather than scarcity, you act more confidently, you ask better questions, you control the process more effectively, you charge more for your product and you see the true value you bring filtered through unencumbered eyes. You give off a certain vibe when you feel abundance that your prospect senses as conviction. And they spend accordingly.

2. **From Low Intent To High Intent:** (From "me first" to "you first.") Your intent influences how you act in the world. You've heard the statistic that 90% of our behavior is subconscious. Think about that for a minute--we aren't even conscious of our own behavior. This goes for the thinking behind what sales is or why we're in it

in the first place. In Chapter 12, we'll talk about High Intent. What you 'intend' determines your actions in the market. Is your intent to 'close the deal' or 'get the business' or 'make quota'? If that is your primary intent then your actions will support that intent. The problem is in the sales process your prospect doesn't care about your quota. They care about their own pains and opportunities. That's why you must radically shift your intent from being a 'me centered intent' to a 'you centered intent.' So I can hear you now saying, "Yes but I still have to make quota." To which I will say, "Yes but quota is a by-product of good intent." Your sale is a **result** of high intent not a driver of high intent. Make your intent about them and their issues—not you and your issues.

3. **From 'I Sell Them' To 'They Sell Me':** (The buyer/ seller dynamic.) The first two fundamental shifts had to do with our thinking but this one has to do with both thinking **and** action. Here's the problem: Most selling approaches are built on the '**convince, persuade and defend**' premise. You know the one that says if you want to sell more, you just convince harder? But that premise is wrong, mainly because it puts the buyer in control. In the old philosophy, the seller sells to the buyer because the buyer has the money and, therefore, the perceived power. Under the new philosophy, **the buyer sells to the seller because the seller has the solution and therefore the control.**

I don't like the 'convince, persuade and defend' sales model. It serves neither the sales person nor the buyer well. When I go to the doctor for an injury, even though I have the money, he has the control. I want my doctor to be in control because he, hopefully, has a solution to my problem. Why is it any different in business-to-business selling?

The customer has the pain. You have the solution. Therefore you should be in control of the sales process. The skill which supports this shift is your effectiveness at creating an environment where the prospect is convincing you that he needs to solve the problem, rather than you convincing him that your product is best.

To which you will say, "Yes, but there are competitors out there who have products equally as good and just because he decides that he has a problem doesn't mean he will choose me to fix it."

To which I will respond, "Yes, but if you are competing on the same level as another vendor then you haven't looked deep enough into your value to differentiate it in the market." When you make that statement, you are concluding you are a commodity (which I am sure you would never openly admit to.) But the point here is that creating an environment where the prospect is selling you on why he needs you to solve his problem—and that he has a problem worth solving—is not created by sales moves or manipulative tactics. It is created by adapting fundamental thinking that unless the customer is truly committed, the solution won't be as valuable.

An Example

I have a client that sells research services to large organizations. They used to sell the old way—cattle calls, blind proposals, RFPs (request for proposals) and 'convince and persuade' sales tactics. Their closing rate was dismal. But now, under the new model, they refuse to make the sale, or even to enter the sales process, if they don't believe that all parties are engaged and committed to some kind of solution. In their world, to try to implement a solution to a bunch of reluctant technicians won't work. The implementation process is too painful. Only when everyone is committed is the value delivered properly. And that happens when the customer is selling them on why they need the solution and why they are ready for it. No more selling.

They do not go to the presentation stage until the buyer is selling them on why they need to solve their problem. And how they've tried to fix it before but it hasn't worked. And how if they don't get this fixed, it will cost them big money. My client has **intentionally** created their selling process to elicit those things. If the buyer isn't selling them, then they leave. Nicely.

Conclusion

So keep these three fundamental shifts in mind. In fact if you go to www.samegamenewrules.com you can download a well designed PDF file that describes these three shifts. It's one you can print, frame and keep in front of you as you sell.

CHANGE STARTS WITH A LOOK IN THE MIRROR

OLD THINKING	NEW THINKING
That psychological babble is for wimps. Popeye said it best: "I y'am what I y'am." If it's not good enough, tough.	I understand that to grow professionally and financially, I must always take inventory of my skills and shortcomings. Only then will I be able to break through to new levels of revenue and income. Change is constant.

All of these insights are about you. We start here because no change occurs until you admit your shortcomings. Ouch! You thought this book was going to be a way to pass a few harmless hours on the subway, right? You didn't think I was going to demand immediate action, did you? Well, it won't take long, but the impact will be enormous.

As you read this, pretend you are with me in one of my workshops. I'm going to ask you the same open-ended questions that we ask our clients. The purpose on any first day in our program is to get you to think, talk and write about the challenges you have in selling that cost you money. The intent is not to make you feel bad or cause you to be upset. There's enough of that in the marketplace. My intent is to help *you* make *you* even better.

> To see what is in front of one's nose requires a constant struggle.
>
> GEORGE ORWELL

Put simply, if you can't admit your problems and are not willing to invest time in continuous improvement, you will never achieve significant growth.

Please answer the questions below. If you are going to be passing this book on and hope for anonymity, then write your responses in your journal or planner. Do write them, though. There are three important reasons for writing these answers out. First, it allows you to switch your role from being observed to being the observer. This enables you to reflect on you. Second, it brings the awareness of the problem from your subconscious mind to your conscious, which is where true problems get acknowledged and solved. Third, writing out your answers will crystallize and clarify areas to work on. It has been said, "Words in writing are the windows to our true thoughts."

> Traditional methods of selling are the embodiment of infringement. When you infringe you drive people away.
>
> BILL CASKEY

#1 Right now, as I look at my annual income, I feel

_____

_____

Here you can answer with one word (happy, sad, content, frustrated), but if you were in my program I wouldn't let you get away with a one word answer. Take some time here. Tell me about it, where it's been and where it's going. Tell me what you'd like it to be and what you would be willing to do to help get it there.

#2 For me, the most anxious moments in selling happen
when _____
_____

Be honest. What bugs you most about the selling process? What bothers you about people, companies, their view of your product or your company—or you? No one will see this. Just get it down on paper.

#3 The main part of the selling process which I would like
to be better at dealing with is _____
_____

Now, this can be the same as #2, but I prefer it be different. Perhaps there is one place where you feel anxiety, and yet another that if you had a magic wand, could wave it and make life grand, this would be it.

A C T I O N   I T E M

Complete the information above. Put it away for two weeks, then get it back out and read it. Let what you wrote make you a little uncomfortable with your current reality. This will start your transformation.

Therapy is over. On with the insights.

INSIGHT TWO

Denial Limits Achievement

OLD THINKING	NEW THINKING
If I can just do the same thing— but do more of it, I can achieve more.	In order for me to get better (higher) results, I must learn to be profoundly more conscious of my behavior and my thoughts.

Denial hinders your achievement on two fronts. One is your own denial about the problems you have in your business. In fact, step one in this book was to get you to become more conscious of those areas that need work. But a second area of denial that will impact you is when your prospect is in denial.

When I first meet salespeople, managers or presidents, I often have to battle through denial or unawareness. When someone sees me coming, even if they've invited me in, their ego still kicks into "protective mode." Here's an example of a client conversation I had last year. Pay close attention to the client's denial of their problem. Also, notice what happens when he opens up and addresses his problem.

Client:	Bill, I'm pretty happy with the way things are right now. I'm not sure there's anything I'd work on in my sales approach.
Me:	Fine, it doesn't sound like we have anything to talk about. Let me ask you this. Do you mean to tell me that you just walk in to your prospect's office and they turn over their checkbook to you? They buy everything from you? They just ask "how much," and write you a check?
Client :	Of course not. That never happens.
Me:	I don't understand. You just told me you don't have any challenges, so I have to assume you close 100% of the deals you work on.
Client :	No way. I close probably 40% of the proposals I do. I don't know anyone who closes 100%.
Me:	But I'm not talking about anyone. I'm talking about you. So what happens in the other 60% of deals that you don't get?
Client :	They buy from someone else or don't buy at all.
Me:	So when do you find out they aren't going to use you? At the beginning, or at the end?
Client:	Usually near the end, after I've quoted and presented.
Me:	So how do you feel about giving away all of that time and expertise and not getting paid for it?
Client:	Not too well, now. I waste a lot of time with people who don't tell me the truth up front.

	Sometimes I find I'm not even talking to the right person. (Beginning to move out of denial.)
Me:	So what does that cost you annually—to have all of these things happen?
Client:	I've never really thought about it like that. It costs me a lot of time that I could be spending with someone else. I probably waste 500 hours a year like that.
Me:	And what is your time worth per hour?
Client:	Based on my income goal, it's probably worth $75-100/hour.
Me:	That's over $40,000. That can't be . . . can it?
Client	Yes, that sounds right.
Me:	So, given that—do you want to work on how to fix that problem?
Client:	Absolutely. I'd be very open to finding out a way to avoid that. (Completely out of denial.)

Do you see how he moved from **denial/unawareness** (I don't have a problem) to **awareness** (I might have a problem) to **acceptance** (I do have a problem that is costing me thousands)? That is the process you must put yourself through if you don't have a coach to help you get there. In this insight, you will learn about the two forms of denial—denial of the problem and denial of the opportunity. You will also learn how to escape your denial and open yourself up for major improvement in your results.

> Those who take up any subject with an open mind, willing to learn anything that will contribute to their advancement, comfort and happiness, are wise.
>
> *JOHN MACDONALD*
> *Message of a Master*

What is denial and what is there about denial that makes it so insidious in our minds? Why is it that we can be achieving at a fraction of our potential, yet our ego won't allow us to acknowledge a different or better tomorrow? Why do we get so enamored with being right that we miss the obvious method to do things better? Is it possible for us to prefer being right to being rich?

> Human beings are perhaps never more frightening than when they are convinced beyond doubt they are right.
>
> *LAURENS VAN DER POST*

Even if we're poor, denial tells us that it's better than the alternative. While drug addicts and alcoholics waste their lives away—losing jobs, marriages, self-esteem, money etc., denial still tells them, "Hey, everything is alright. Don't worry. Just keep doing what you're doing. There's no reason to change."

That's why denial is insidious—because it won't allow you to look at the problem through a clear set of glasses. So why does denial hinder achievement?

I've had thousands of people in my programs during the past 16 years and I can tell you one common belief of the people who make the most progress in self-development—they are open to examining how they think, and they are open to changing them if they believe new thoughts work better.

> Comfort comes as a guest, lingers to become a host and stays to enslave us.
>
> *LEE BICKMORE*

Conversely, the common theme among the strugglers is: "I'm doing alright now. Everything will work out. Don't try to change my habits. How I think is my identity. Leave me alone."

Denial is the ego's way of telling you that everything you're doing now is right and there's no reason to change. It can work in two ways—denial of a problem or denial of an opportunity. Let's explore the first form of denial—denial of the problem, with an example to illustrate.

Denial of Problem

In June of 1996, a company came to me with the task of improving their revenue results in the Central Region. They had been growing at an eight percent annual pace, while the market had been growing at twenty percent per year. They were mystified. Upon careful personal assessment through interviews with each salesperson, I found these people were in tremendous denial about the real problem. They blamed their mediocre performance on external issues—they didn't have laptop computers, pricing was too high, too many reports they had to file, poor market demand, etc., Call them excuses or denial, but they weren't dealing with the real issue—their approach in selling their product. It was extremely weak and disorganized. It was actually quite remarkable they were doing as well as they were. Their selling skills were mediocre and they were unwilling to accept it.

> On this earth, in the final analysis, each of us gets exactly what he deserves. But only the successful recognize this.
>
> GEORGES SIMEON

In this specific case, denial of the real issue was costing the company ten million dollars per year and costing each of the reps $75-100,000 in income.

Until they were able to look at their specific core problems, and look at the impact that their denial was having on their income, no solution would be acceptable. They would continue to look to the external environment as being responsible for their sluggish performance. Here is the rule you should follow:

R U L E

When you look externally for the cause of the problem, you limit your ability to fix it.

Once I began asking them questions, posing other pos-sibilities to them, and taking them to task on their thinking, we made progress. Once they were willing to emerge from denial into taking complete responsibility for their results, they empowered themselves to change.

Denial of Opportunity

More hideous than denial of our problems is the fact that many of us, including me, are in denial of the true oppor-tunity that we have in business. In a way, this can have even more drastic impact because it takes some work to bring it to consciousness. Here is a story that illustrates this point.

Jim came to me in the fall of 1997. He was a sales rep with a high-end telecommunications company ($200,000+ systems). His denial took on a different flavor. He acknowl-edged that he had selling prob-lems, which is how he ended up in the program. But what he couldn't come to terms with was the vast market opportunity that existed for him. He was totally blind to it—either purposely or unconsciously. He was earning $75,000 and could have been earning $200-500,000 if he would have changed his perception.

> Nothing in life is to be feared.
> It is only to be understood.
>
> *MARIE CURIE*

He had a franchise of technology that no one else had. And because his market was abundant, he could have hired five junior sales agents to sell in his territory. Instead he chose to remain in the "I'm just a sales rep" mode.

Sometimes "denial of opportunity" is a safe place for us to hide because it protects us from being too successful. Expectation levels don't get heightened and disappoint-ment doesn't ensue when we fall short. So, instead, we deny the massive opportunity which exists by refusing even to look at a new potential. This is what traps people into Old Thinking.

Both of these denials—pain and opportunity—are important. So let's start this book of insights by bringing them to the surface and helping you become conscious. Where is your denial? Is it in how you're doing things currently? Have you looked recently at your selling processes? Have you looked at your results? Have you looked at your income-producing strategies and isolated the problems or challenges both for your personal income and your company's? Have you taken an in-depth inventory of your skills in business and created a plan to improve them?

Next, have you looked at your markets in a way that would enable you to open up large amounts of opportunity by reframing your view of the world? Is there a way to generate alliances with competitive vendors? Denial will tell you that idea "just won't work." Is there a way to generate alliances with others who sell to the same customers you do? Denial will tell you, "they would never go for that." Is there a way to reposition your approach to your market that would totally change the reaction you get from your prospects? Would that re-positioning create a rush of new opportunities you aren't getting now? Denial will tell you, "That's someone else's job, not mine. I'm just a sales rep."

> Change your thoughts and you change your world.
>
> NORMAN VINCENT PEALE

Actually, we all slip into unconsciousness in our business lives because there are probably parts of our lives which don't work well—or as well as they could. When we become conscious of those problems or opportunities, we have two choices: look away (which is easier), or look deeper (which is what I hope this book will get you to do). When we look deeper, we always become more honest with ourselves, by engaging in **empowering thinking** rather than avoidance thinking.

With **empowering thinking**, solutions begin to reveal themselves. Tactics become real and your confidence soars as the world becomes abundant. Acceptance of reality is a key to abundant thinking.

So as you read these insights and as they speak to you personally, check out in your own gut whether denial plays a part. If you feel a gut con-

> We visit others
> as a social obligation.
> How long has it been since
> we've visited ourselves?
>
> *MORRIS ADLER*

nection with an insight, your soul may be saying, "There's something here; check it out," which in turn will shift your consciousness into looking for a solution, rather than covering up a problem.

Conclusion

I want you to achieve profound success in business, in selling, and in life. I want your life to be even more enriched than it is now. My hope is that you'll be honest with yourself and keep your ego at bay long enough for these insights to enter your mind at a deeper level and foster an environment which will prime the pump for life-long personal development.

Once you decide to tear down the wall of denial, don't fool yourself into thinking the job is done. Be conscious of what you have chosen to face and accept. Then, be aware when the symptoms of denial begin to return in these areas, because you will again be limiting your revenue and opportunities. After all, denial is an expensive habit. In the previous example, it was costing Jim $75,000 a year. What is it costing you?

A C T I O N   I T E M

In the space below, write what you believe about selling, achievement, business and anything else that comes to mind. Writing is your best method of discovering your core beliefs. This writing doesn't need to be long and epic. Just a paragraph on each of the areas you want to improve. Then, find a colleague to do the same exercise and act as "cross-mentors" for each other. Have them challenge you on why you believe such things and you challenge them on their beliefs. You may find you're both in denial of current conditions or of future opportunities. This will be a way to keep you awake and enlightened to potential denials or opportunities. Keep this notebook for future reference. This is the time to be brutally honest with yourself.

Selling _____

_____

_____

Achievement _____

_____

_____

Business _____

_____

_____

(____) _____

_____

_____

INSIGHT THREE

PROCESS MAKES PERFECT

OLD THINKING	NEW THINKING
My prospect decides when, what and how much.	I decide when, what and how much.

Here's something you may not have read before. *Engineers make the best salespeople.*

The reason is because they are process people and process thinkers. They are able to take a product from concept to design to production. They understand the problems inherent in any process, and they understand the dynamics in getting those problems solved. They know intuitively from their training that "A" has to happen before "B," which has to happen before "C." If they are going to go down the path of "C," then they have to make sure "A" and "B" are complete.

When I talk about *process* in selling, I am talking about the process which begins when the dialogue starts and ends—not when the PO is signed, but when the solution is complete.

> Respect yourself if you would
> have others respect you.
>
> *BALTASAR GRACIAN*
> *The Art of Worldly Wisdom*

I want to help you develop a method of creating and communicating your value that empowers you to control the sales and evaluation process—not necessarily the prospect's decision process. I also want you to be able to lay out your process to the unenlightened so that they can follow you.

If you can put enough people into your sales process and create environments where that process will lead to outcomes, even if the outcome is "no," then you will achieve great success. However, when you either engage too few people in your process or are unable to work them through it, then you limit your income potential.

Here is an example: We have a computer software company that works with us. When we first began, they were having trouble moving prospects through their process.

> A little system prevents
> a lot of bungling.
>
> *Oxford Dictionary*
> *for American Proverbs*

They would get hung up half way through and deals would fall through. So, I played "prospect" once in a role play and it became grossly evident what was happening. They weren't helping the prospect. They had absolutely no process laid out to help the prospect buy. After weeks of working, here is what we coached them to say on the first call:

Mark, thanks for your interest in the software system. Can I take a few minutes and lay out the process that seems to have worked for some of our other clients? I thought we could spend today talking about why you were interested, and what business problems you have in your Information Services department. Then at the end of this meeting, we can decide if we want to go further. If we decide not to advance this, then neither of us will have wasted any time. If we decide to move forward, I'll probably need to speak with your management team and find out what their issues are. Then if we want to continue after that, you and I can get back together and plan the process from there. Does that sound appropriate?

> The eagle who soars in the upper air does not worry itself as to how to cross rivers. Therefore, think higher.

Then, throughout the sale, practice what we call "**orientation**." This is the act of laying out your process each step of the way. On the first call, lay out an overview of the entire cycle. Or, if you're already five calls into the process, then take the next logical number of calls and lay them out. You must always be orienting your prospect to what your process is.

This works extremely well if you're in a cycle that is either long, or confusing or both.

> Courage is contagious. When a brave man takes a stand, the spines of others are stiffened.
>
> REV. BILLY GRAHAM

You can't blame the prospect for not following your process if he doesn't know what it is. If your prospect doesn't buy your product often (less than once per month) or hasn't changed vendors in a while, then orientation is a "must."

A C T I O N   I T E M

In your next five sales calls take a risk and *orient* your prospect to your process from here on. By doing that, you will start to control the process. If your buyer asks for something that you're not ready to give him yet—like a proposal—simply lay out your process and tell him when you'll give it to him.

DETACHMENT INCREASES YOUR POWER

OLD THINKING	NEW THINKING
Yes is good. No is bad. Think it over means there is still a chance.	I work my process with conviction and diligence, and expend no energy worrying about outcomes. I am here to find and solve problems—not force behavior.

When I introduce the concept of detachment at my work-shops, I get a room full of blank stares. The concept, while powerful, transgresses what we've been trained to believe as salespeople. Moreover, it's inconsistent with what we learned as children. The best way for me to share with you the power of detachment is to tell you the true story of Jill.

Jill came to me as a salaried salesperson for a landscaping company. She was earning $30,000 a year and happy with herself, but not thrilled about the job. She ended up taking another sales position in a highly competitive marketplace. After she struggled for a few months, we sat down and talked. What I found was not unusual. Since she had no experience in commission sales, she became extremely attached to each deal. The bigger the deal got, the more attached she became. Moreover, the more needy she appeared in front of her prospect, the less risk she was likely to take in the sales process.

> Never contend with a man who has nothing to lose.
>
> BALTASAR GRACIAN

She couldn't even bring herself to ask the questions that she had to know prior to proceeding. It was as if she thought every prospect she had was the last one on the planet. Intellectually she knew that wasn't the case, but emotionally, she was unable to detach. When she got so hung up emotionally on whether she made the sale or not, her power would slip. Her manager didn't help much. He placed high-levels of pressure on her when she didn't "get the deal."

We worked for a few months on the condition. It was tough work. It challenged her core thoughts and beliefs about selling and achievement. She had always been taught to hold on tight to everything. But eventually Jill was able to detach. She arrived at a new point where she cared slightly less about making the sale than the customer did about solving the problem. She had a tremendous energy to help people solve their problems, but her new rules dictated that she couldn't care more than they did. The end result? Her income doubled within six months. The last time I spoke with Jill, she was on her way to $100,000 a year. And she'll tell you the rise in income was due to detachment.

Unfortunately, detachment and the ability to let go are not natural characteristics in any of us. From the time we were kids we were taught to hang on to what we had. If you have any doubt about that, watch three-year-olds play together. There is a constant tug of war between what one has and what the other one wants. We acquire our identity, in part, by what we possess. And when someone takes something from us that we perceive as being ours, it feels like they're taking part of us. This is also a cul-

> Absolute detachment is a polar region unfit for human life; but one might well get out of the steaming jungles and come a bit closer to the pole.
>
> CRANE BRINTON

tural dilemma. When we have so much of ourselves tied up in what we own, and our "stuff," then we naturally protect our "stuff" by clutching it.

We learn early that when someone takes a thing from us, we lose and they win. But in sales, this antiquated thinking hurts us. I like Catherine Ponder's many examples in her book *Open Your Mind To Prosperity*. She says:

> When you are trying to achieve a result and it has not come, it is often because there is still something in mind, body or affairs . . . that you need to renounce, free, release or eliminate. As long as you put off this elimination process, you put off results. Elimination not only takes something from you, it gives you something.

In sales we hang on to things much too long. We have deals that we work on for months and then we can't figure out why we can't get new deals into our pipeline. The problem begins when we attach ourselves emotionally to the deals we have. It prohibits us from asking the questions we need to ask to preserve our own dignity like, "are we going to do this or not?"

Consequently, for any type of sales professional, detachment is a very difficult attitude to adopt. We're attached to whether we get to work on time, to whether people approve of us, to whether we get an appointment from a prospect and to whether the prospect buys. Then, we go to sales training and are told "you can sell anybody anything if you just sell harder." Do you see the prob-

> Man can learn nothing except by going from the known to the unknown.
>
> *CLAUDE BERNARD*

lem? When your emotional energy is attached to a deal you're working on, how many prospects are you passing by? How many potential clients are you ignoring because your sights are set too narrowly on this one prospect—leaving you blind to what's happening around you? Attachment causes tunnel vision.

In game six of the 1998 NBA Finals, Chicago Bulls Coach Phil Jackson was asked by a reporter what he told his team before the game. He quoted an old Buddhist saying, "I told them to chop wood, carry water." Considering Jackson's background in Zen philosophies, his response isn't surprising. What Jackson meant was this: "We'll go out and work hard, do the things we need to do, each play our role, and not make it more complicated than it has to be. We chop wood. We carry water. We play the game minute by minute but we detach from the outcomes."

In sales, what that really means is, do what you can, learn all you can, go out to the marketplace and generate activity. But remember, at the end of the day, the outcome is the outcome. Don't worry about the outcome.

Practicing Detachment in Business

In the sales game, you should always tell the prospect up front some variation of "It's OK if you don't buy from me," or "It's OK if you say no." That portrays detachment. When you approach a prospect from that position, it appears on the surface that you're giving away control and power, but you are surrendering to outcomes which puts you in a higher state of control—not only of the process but of your own emotions and destiny.

R U L E

Never be a hostage to your emotional needs.

R U L E

Never make your prospect a hostage to those needs either.

Because this is such a different way of thinking and looking at achievement, we need to create a process that automatically engages this thinking in your mind. That's why in Insight 3, you heard us talk about the process. The process acts as a filter *in* which you engage people, and *from* which you cut people. It is the process you create to help you detach from any outcome. If

> Wisdom consists of passing up nonessentials.

you can engage enough people in enough activity, then you really and truly will not care about the outcome of any one prospect because you have enough people engaged to make your numbers.

HERE'S AN EXAMPLE

Let's suppose that 80% of the time when you involve the president of a company in your sales process, you close the business and are able to provide the optimum solution for the client. And only 20% of the time when the president is absent do you get the sale. Overall, your odds increase 400% when the president is involved.

Let's also suppose you're now in a process where the VP of Operations has told you right up front that the president will not be involved in this process. You know that your odds just dropped 400%. You now have a choice to make. Do you continue through the process knowing your odds of closing this will be a fraction of what they could be? Or do you create an environment where you force the prospect to make a decision and if he doesn't want the president involved, you're not willing to go any further? In this respect, the prospect makes the decision for you. If he still maintains the president doesn't want to get involved, then you kindly, willingly and gently, but assertively, pack up your bags and leave the process.

> When I call on a client,
> I come by cab and I am sleek
> and clean and four square.
> I carry myself as though I've
> made a quiet killing on the
> stock market, and have come
> to call more as a public service
> than anything else.
>
> *KURT VONNEGUT*
> Welcome to the Monkey House

Now remember, before you tell me that you'd never do that because the chance to close is at least two out of ten, you must believe you have an abundant market. You know you can only work with a certain number of prospects at one time. So the fact that this one person doesn't want to do anything is OK. You're detached. And you are detached not because you don't care, but because you only want to help people who are willing to engage in your rules.

When you're doing the right things up front in the sales process, the prospect is less likely to let you go because of a minor thing (like the president's involvement). Through your ability to detach from the outcome, the prospect sees your convictions, senses you know what you're doing, and is likely to change their rules accordingly.

The Words to Say

I know this is a stretch for some of you, but stay with me. When you're detached from the outcome in the sales process, you will instinctively know what to say, how to say it, and when to say it, because you'll be acting from your intuition rather than from your ego. Bear in mind these words may not be exactly how they will come out for you, but hear the concept at work.

When you're detached you can say the following things:

- "I'm not sure if I can help you."
- "It doesn't sound like you really need me. Sounds like you have everything under control."
- "If we can't get the President and Operations Manager involved, I'm not sure there is a point in continuing."
- "I've been sitting for an hour listening to you, and I really don't hear the things that most prospects tell me at this point. Have I missed something?"
- "If you have such a good relationship with your current vendor, why am I here?"

I'm not recommending you say these exact things or say them all at once, I'm only suggesting that you cannot say these if you're attached to a "yes" answer at the end of the sale.

Remember, detachment does not mean cavalier or cocky. Actually it is just the opposite. Your regard for their problem is so high that if you see they care less than you do, you must conserve your energy and walk away, and look for someone who is serious about solving their problem. The caring is not just about you caring for them—it is about *you* caring for *you*. But when you walk—never walk in contempt—never from a place of anger or disdain. A paradox remains—there is a leap of faith that must occur for a salesperson to adopt this approach. Moreover, detachment without the corresponding techniques and strategies that we're putting forth here will be seen as manipulative and ineffective.

The result of detachment is a form of courage. The strength it gives to you actually attracts people at a psychological level. When you come from a place of strength and detachment, more and more prospects see you as something (or someone) they need. More and more clients want to do additional business with you. More sales processes go your way.

Detachment does not mean uncaring. It does not mean you don't want to make quota. It means you're OK either way. You have an ultimate belief in abundance and any lack or shortcoming you experience is only temporary.

A C T I O N   I T E M

To change your income and grow, you must constantly be filling your funnel up with bigger and better opportunities. One way to do this is to release some smaller fish. Go through your client list and your funnel. Get rid of the ones that are too small for you or haven't had any positive movement in the last thirty days. Make this a ritual.

Always clean your closet and throw away the dated items. Detach.

Vision Strengthens Your Inner Game

OLD THINKING	NEW THINKING
I just have to gather it up and be tougher—you know—have more courage. Sometimes I just need to do the things I don't want to do.	It's all about creatively picturing and building the vision I want in my life. Only after I create my personal vision will I be able to move effortlessly through the marketplace.

Everyone talks about goals. When I begin my workshops, I always ask people, "Do you have goals?" "Yes!" they shout in unison. It seems like the right answer to the question—or the right thing to say in a workshop. But then I step up the pressure. "What do your goals sound like? Can you state them without looking at your planner? What is the most inspiring goal you have?" When I ask those questions, I get empty looks, worried stares and wimpy answers. People even look away from me—trying to avoid eye contact.

I've concluded that we've all been misled by the hype around goal setting. I bought into it, too, when I started my training business in 1989. I had a mentor who was a believer in "cookbook training." Cookbook training amounts to identifying the daily behavior needed to be successful in your business and then executing and tracking it. It all sounds good.

> Every man takes the limits
> of his own field of vision
> for the limits of the world.
>
> ARTHUR SCHOPENHAUER

Here's how it works. "I need to generate $1M in sales which means I need 25 more accounts. To do that, I must quote 100 cases (deals). Since my numbers show I must talk to five suspects for every quote, I need to have 500 first appointments. In order to do that, I've got to make 5000 phone calls. Since I have 230 working days per year, that means 25 calls per day."

On paper it sounds awesome. You can get rich by doing this exercise. However, there's more to it than that. If that was all there was to it, lead generation would be easy. But it isn't. In fact, if you walk into the sales war rooms of 1000 companies and ask them what their biggest problem in sales is, a high percentage would say "lead generation."

So why is it that by the end of the first week in January, I'm off my goal? By the end of the first month, I'm so far behind I have no hope of catching up. The reason is that in the vast majority of cases, and in mine too, I spent way too much time with the calculator, dividing, multiplying and running the numbers to arrive at what my daily behavior needed to be. And way too little time creating the picture or the vision of what I really wanted.

What compounds the problem when there is little time invested up front in your vision, is that you will spend the rest of your life chasing behavior that may not be in line with what you want to achieve in the long term. In other words, when there is no clear vision, how do you know you're doing the right things on a daily basis?

Maybe instead of making 20 cold calls a day, you should be out looking for a business alliance that feeds leads to you. Instead of sending out 5000 direct mail pieces each month, maybe you should be generating referrals by visiting your current clients. With no visions, who is to say you're utilizing your assets in the right place?

> In dreams begin
> our possibilities.
>
> **WILLIAM SHAKESPEARE**

Faith in the Market

My experience with high-achieving people tells me that there's a certain amount of faith you must put in the marketplace to attract the things that will help you achieve your vision. Within your personal vision are the tools and assets needed to accomplish that vision. Your mind won't allow you to create a vision or a picture of the future if you don't have the ability to accomplish it. Napoleon Hill said, "Whatever the mind of man can conceive, it can also achieve." And the converse is true.

> When someone says,
> "I know this sounds crazy,
> but . . . " rest assured you are
> closing in on their vision.
>
> **RICK JAROW**

Impact of No Vision

What happens if you're in selling or business development and you take no time to build a picture of your future reality? Many things. Let's look at three and you check those that apply in your life.

1. With No Vision, Good Decisions Are Hard to Make

Every decision that passes in front of you as a seller becomes monumental. Details begin to overwhelm you. You will work through the marketplace as a rudderless ship with no aim, no direction, and with everything looking good to you. And because you have no "end in mind," you have no coherent vision of what your perfect future will look like. And when there is no vision, you will end up chasing deals and opportunities that will actually hold you back from accomplishing something larger and greater. This "noise" will prevent you from getting closer to your vision. Without a vision, you won't have a guidepost to which to look as you decide what action to take in the marketplace.

> Planning, when too tightly controlled and goal-oriented does not allow space for the creative. Most goal-oriented people place a high value on outcomes because they still see themselves enmeshed in poverty.
>
> *RICK JAROW*

Have you ever watched someone struggle when they didn't have a clear picture of their future? Watch people who can't make decisions. You probably have them in your company. Hopefully, they aren't running your company. Watch people struggle with the minutiae of decisions that need to be made and realize that it isn't the decision that's the problem, it's the lack of vision.

2. With No Vision, Courage Suffers

When you have no picture of your future, you sacrifice the courage to make the tough decisions. You get wimpy. You will spend too much time with people who will never buy. You'll seldom challenge people, preferring to accept at face value all they say. Those tough conversations that you know you need to have with your spouse, your assistants, your customer service person, your top client and your manager, all become tougher to have. Moreover, you will not demand to see the people who have the problems—the decision-makers. You can talk all day about calling on the VIP, but if you don't have the courage, you ain't gonna make the call. And if you don't have the vision, you aren't going to muster up that courage.

3. WITHOUT VISION, YOUR MENTAL TOUGHNESS WANES

Along with the courage problem above, you also have another issue. When the tough times hit, and they will, it becomes harder to pick yourself up and get back on the horse. Lack of vision leads to a self-consciousness that stops you from taking risks and being laser focused. All in all, your mental toughness is like a muscle—without use, it atrophies.

> Dream lofty dreams and as you dream, so shall you become. Your vision is the promise of what you shall one day be.
>
> *JAMES ALLEN*
> As a Man Thinketh

So What Does a Clear Vision Look Like?

For the sake of brevity, this book is about your achievement in selling and business, so let's limit your vision to several things:

1. The income you would like to see on your W-2.
2. The types of companies you would like to work with (as a salesperson or business owner).
3. The optimum process you will engage in with those prospects.

Stories are the best method of illustrating the power of vision, so here is one that happened to me a couple of years ago.

Jerry was 45 years old and had been in the same position in his company for over five years. An account executive calling on mid-sized accounts in the northeast, he was earning a decent income—$90,000 with some perks. Everything was going OK, but, like most of us, he had dreams that were never going to be accomplished if he stayed for another five years. And like most of us, he was never asked by his superiors what those dreams were.

Don't get me wrong. He liked what he did. He loved the company and the industry, but he knew there was more. In his case, part of the problem was that his company wasn't helping him set any kind of personal vision. All they cared about was "what are you bringing in this month?" If his vision was going to happen, it would be up to him to create it— exactly the way it should be.

> When you cease to dream, you cease to live.
>
> MALCOLM FORBES

I sat with Jerry for an hour one day and posed questions to him that no one, as far as he could recall, had ever asked him. The first question I asked was this: "Jerry, it's five years from now. Tell me about the ideal life that you've created."

After a couple of false starts—with him trying to tell me what that life looked like—he finally resigned to me, "I just can't do it. I have no idea what I want it to look like. I guess that's my problem. I have no goals." "No," I replied, "Goals aren't the answer. Goals don't paint a picture. Goals are those temporary stops on the way to your vision. They aren't your vision. Until you get clear on what you want your business life to look like, you simply won't get there. In fact, right now there are probably opportunities swirling around you that you don't even see because you haven't built your vision."

Vision does that for us. It allows us to see things that are invisible. It allows us to have a sense of confidence that whatever we conceive our future to be, we can make it so.

Jerry's New Vision

When Jerry and I were finished, he had created a clear vision in three areas—income, account size and optimum process. I'll share with you what those were.

INCOME

He was earning $90,000 a year plus perks. By the year 2004 (five years out) he wanted to be earning $250,000 a year. He said he wasn't sure how that was going to happen, since he was currently the top performer at his company. He also became nervous about how he was going to accomplish that from a time standpoint—he was already working 12-hour days. But I told him you can't worry about the tactics—forget HOW it's going to happen. Your goal is to contemplate, reflect and connect with that number. It will happen, if you will only invest some time in it and have faith in the market to supply it to you. But you need to set it forth because without a consciousness of it, the Universe has no way of knowing what it needs to provide for you. "If you're going to ask the marketplace to supply you with a $160,000 pay increase, you, at the very least, need to give it a chance to help you by being specific."

> We have forgotten the age-old fact that God speaks chiefly through dreams and visions.
>
> CARL JUNG

ACCOUNT TYPE

Currently, his average account size was $50,000 a year (in purchases from his company). His vision was very simple—in five years he wanted to be working with only 15 accounts that were buying at least $100,000 a year of products. That would be enough for him. He might even have to hire a junior account person to work on details of the accounts. But he was OK with that. In fact, the more we talked about that, the more invigorated he became at the thought of bringing someone else in and teaching him the business.

But as most people do, he started to resist the vision. "But, my company has never brought in junior people before. I'm not so sure they'd go for that." I had to stop him again. "Remember, Jerry, this is your personal vision. You are not prepared right now to assess the tactics or the strategy of how this will happen. You must put faith in your mind to make it work." Jerry was beginning to do what most do during the vision creation process—look at why it won't work.

Another part of his vision in this area was "whom he was calling on." Right now, he was calling too far down the food chain within his client companies. Sure, he was still achieving at an OK level, but whenever a problem would arise, he found he had no direct line to a chief executive to help get it solved. Plus, there were several of his accounts where he knew he could solve more problems for them (sell them more), but because he couldn't get to the right people, he was unable to advance deals. He ended up wasting a lot of precious time making presentations to people who couldn't say "yes"— who could only say "no." He set out, as part of his vision, that he would not make any presentations prior to seeing the Chief Executive Officer.

> To know what you prefer instead of humbly saying Amen to what the world says you ought to prefer, is to have kept your soul alive.
>
> ROBERT LOUIS STEVENSON

With this account vision settled, we moved to his vision of the optimum process.

Optimum Process

Along with seeing the chief officer of his prospect organization, he also insisted on a specific process to follow as part of his vision. Currently, when he would begin conversation with a company, he would wander all around in the organization—never knowing what land mine he was going to step on next. Often, he found himself walking on eggshells, unsure and unaware of any of their internal processes. And since he had no sales process of his own, he became a hostage to their buying cycle.

His new vision was going to fix that. He would have a three-step process to help him determine if he wanted to work with these prospects. He laid it out to me quite eloquently. It contained one or two up-front meetings, an assessment step where he would do a formal problem-assessment, and a formal presentation step with a decision to be made by the prospect at the end of the demonstration. It was elegant, simple and would cut his selling costs in half. He knew he would have to have such a process if he were to work with high-performance companies and do so in a timely basis.

> Look and you will find it—what is unsought will go undetected.
>
> SOPHOCLES

He also needed to spend his time servicing his existing clients—not spending hundreds of hours in the selling process. In fact, another part of his "process vision" was to spend 75% of his time calling on his current clients—finding out what their problems were and how he could help them, thereby growing his income too. He was familiar with the #1 Law of Marketing—it is easier to sell current clients than new prospects. And luckily, he had more to sell them.

In fact it was so simple for him to articulate this visionary process to me, I asked why he hadn't put it in place already.

He said what most people say: "I've never looked at it in this light before. I've never looked at it as part of a vision that was going to get me to my ideal future."

As we finished, a smile came over his face. His eyes held an energy they didn't have before. He didn't seem so beaten down. He seemed to have a direction and an aim now.

The result?

I called him one year after our meeting and asked him what had happened. He was ecstatic. He said that almost immediately, after our session, he began calling on larger accounts. He didn't have to *force* himself to do it like he had prior to our meeting and this exercise. He just naturally gravitated there. He wasn't nervous—he had no fear. He didn't have to force his way in. Plus, he found himself in the president's office more often. He didn't feel like he was going over anyone's head to do it. He just called higher. He also had increased his average customer size by 30%. So in just 12 months he was 30% of the way to the vision. Not once did he sit down and do any kind of a behavioral plan.

Jerry found what most people discover during this exercise. When you set the vision and paint the perfect picture, and do it in a way that correlates to your values, you will reap rewards sooner, rather than later. Once the vision is put out to the consciousness, it begins immediately to attract the tools necessary for its achievement.

A C T I O N   I T E M

Do something similar to what Jerry did in the above example. Begin talking, writing or drawing about those three vision areas—*income, clients, processes,* and get clear about what your ideal future would look like.

You might even do what we ask our clients to do—get three blank sheets of paper, go off for a few hours to your private castle, and begin to write and dream. Devote one piece of paper to each of the three areas. Only you can do this. Don't go with a group. Don't tell anyone where you're off to. This is a private meeting between you and you. When you begin to blab about what you're doing or bragging about it, your ego will sabotage you. You'll start to look for approval from outside sources and it won't be there. So quietly, move off into your inner world and work on your personal vision.

At that meeting, ask yourself some deep questions—what do I want my business life to look like in five years? Why do I want it to look that way? What are some things I want to pull into my life to support my values and me? What do I want my income to be? What type of business relationships (clients or customers) do I want to have? Complete the sentence stem "I know this sounds crazy, but. . . . " And don't for an instant wonder "what will my manager think?" or "what will my husband think?" This is your vision—no one else's.

THE MOST SUCCESSFUL SALESPEOPLE ENGAGE IN CONCERTED MARKET ACTIVITY

OLD THINKING	NEW THINKING
It's up to my marketing and promotion departments to create leads for me.	"If it is to be, it is up to me." I take full responsibility for learning how to engage in the kind of market activity that will help me generate the income I deserve.

How does a person go from annual earnings of $65,000 to over $150,000 after only one year's work? It happened to Al—and it could happen to you. He did it by engaging in a process called Concerted Market Activity (CMA). CMA is the combination of activities in your market, which stirs people to speak with you about your solution.

Here is Al's story:

If you've ever been in the commercial insurance business you know how brutally competitive it is. Every prospect in the city is being called on by at least five other agents. It seems like everyone has a brother-in-law in that business. Al came to me with a problem. He wanted to earn more money, but was having tremendous difficulty finding prospects. As we talked, I could see there were three problems.

First, he was waiting on his marketing department to put enough leads in front of him to make him wealthy. That wasn't working. Seldom is any marketing department able to do that. The leads they were giving him were quite worthless—too low on the food chain and not in enough pain. There was no compelling reason for them to change. So the first thing he had to do was think of himself not as a salesperson, but as a marketer.

Second, Al had to take ongoing, consistent action in the marketplace—the Concerted Market Activity mentioned above. He had to realize that to get from $65,000 to his goal of $150,000 he would have to spend a lot less time with the masses and a lot more time on the select few who had com-

> No great man ever complains of want of opportunity.
>
> *RALPH WALDO EMERSON*

pelling reasons to work with him. But to do that, he had to have a plan and stick to it—no matter what. He had to know the numbers. Ultimately, Al needed to know how many deals he had to close, and from there, back in to the numbers and types of behaviors necessary to make it so.

Third, he felt like he was being held hostage by his prospects for better deals, more discounts and, most often, just being fed lies and stalls. He never felt like he could disqualify people (fire them) and move on because he never had enough in his new business pipeline. It was a constant hostage situation and he was finding it impossible to stay detached enough (Insight 4) to ask the tough questions and see the right people. Each night he would go home with a knot in his stomach wondering if tomorrow would be better.

So, I said, "Al, you've got to get out of this hostage situation. There's only one way to do it. And that is to have enough new prospects in your funnel that you can fire any-one of them and feel OK. You also need a philosophy to help you do the right things on a daily, weekly and monthly basis to get where you want to go." He agreed. Here's what he came up with.

Assessment

First I asked him to assess how he got his last twenty-five clients. This would give him a 30,000-foot view of his business and his new business-acquisition process. Believe it or not, his company, like most others, had never done that. Did his new business come via call in, cold call, an article in the newspaper, or internal marketing department? What activity was working to provide a stream of prospects?

> When you need a friend is no time to make one.
>
> *MARK TWAIN*

By doing this, he determined what kind of consistent behavior was needed to raise his odds of repeating the successful results. He found some startling statistics. Just three streams of activities produced those twenty-five clients. In descending order, they were 1) referrals from existing clients, 2) free speeches to civic clubs and 3) informal networking. So I told him to forget every other activity his boss was asking him to do, including cold calls, writing articles for the paper (which weren't even getting published) and letter writing (a worthless activity in this business). He put together a monthly plan at the end of every month, which laid out his behavior for the next month. This was done to effectively engage in those three activities.

LEVERAGE YOUR STRENGTH

One of the things he really liked was visiting with current clients. He was very personable and everyone liked to see him coming. But I asked him to do something else besides just visit. I asked him to bring value in some way. Bring a book, a tape, a lead, a different way to solve an insurance problem—something that they could point to and say, "Al is really helping our business." He actually generated a small monograph book titled "11 Ways To Save Money On Insurance," produced it for less than $500 and gave it to his existing clients on his visits. It was also something he could send to the referrals they gave him.

> Chance is always powerful.
> Let your hook be always cast;
> in the pool where you least
> expect it, there will be a fish.
>
> OVID

He also made a list of the civic clubs he could speak to. He drew circles of his informal networks to better visualize how many people he really knew in his region. Then he could see a visual of what he needed to do at the beginning of each month. His goals were as follows.

Meet with five current clients a month; book three free speeches, even if they were to a retired ladies bridge party; and ask five people to lunch from his informal network (but only to bring them value, not to ask for referrals). As part of the tactic, he was not allowed to ask or beg, as he had in the past, for referrals. He had a detailed and meticulous script, which followed many of the tactics within these insights.

GET UNATTACHED

As part of his training, he had to stay unattached to any and all outcomes. He could not "sell" in the traditional sense of the word. He was a prospector—much like the gold prospectors in the 1800s—using sifters to pan for gold. He was using Concerted Market Activity to pan for a similar gold and it worked. Here are the results.

It was three months before he had his first new client and it was only a small one. But he continued the behavior. Every month—five client meetings, three free speeches and five lunches with his informal network. By the sixth month, he had picked up five new clients, one of which became his largest. And by the eleventh month he had twelve new clients, all of whom have remained with him to this printing.

His income, which had been stagnant at $65-70,000 for the previous five years, had shot up to $120,000. With a small change in his attitude and a big change in behavior, he had profoundly increased his income. He was concerted in his activity and disciplined in his behavior—and he profited from his plan.

A man who does not leave his hut will bring nothing in.

WEST AFRICAN PROVERB

So what really happened to Al? Was there more to the story? If the plan was that simple, why had he struggled for so many years? All good questions.

Here's the thing most people miss. Al wasn't going to change his results until his behavior changed and that wasn't going to change until his mind-set changed. He had to develop new rules to live by. The primary thought-change he experienced was that he was no longer dependent upon his marketing department for prospect generation. If he was to quantum leap his income, it was up to him. Second, his new rule of thought was that he was marketer first and seller second. And third, he didn't really care who bought from him. He didn't give two bits about the outcome of any call, of any deal, of any quote, of any speech. He only cared about his disciplined behavior in those three areas of market activity. He managed his own behavior and allowed the Universe to do the rest.

The key thing to know is that he never felt pressure. He never put pressure on himself or on the prospect. He was just moving through the marketplace—chopping wood, carrying water and letting the chips fall. They fell all right— smack in his pocket.

WHAT ABOUT YOU?

So what about your streams of activity? Have you put all your eggs in one basket—having one thing that works for you and none other? Or have you taken Al's path and assessed your business? Have you looked at your business like a business and not like a sales territory? After you kiss the kids good night and doze off, do you do so with a profound certainty that tomorrow you will harvest the crop you planted last month? And what are your activity streams? We recommend you have at least three that you work diligently. We've listed a few below with brief descriptions. Sure, you've heard all of this before, but if you don't have people beating your door down to do business with you, then perhaps it would be wise to read over them.

> The heights of great men reached and kept; Were not attained by sudden flight; But they, while their companions slept; Were toiling upward in the night.
>
> **HENRY WADSWORTH LONGFELLOW**
> *The Ladder of St. Augustine*

Referrals

This is the most overlooked stream of prospecting—mainly because it is difficult to ask your current clients for names of people they know. So, try this instead. Schedule a meeting with your top 10 clients and tell them this: *"I'm looking at growing my business in this area. One thing I could do is advertise and use direct mail to build my business. But it just doesn't seem economically smart to do that when I have good clients like you who probably know people whom I could help. So, I'd like to tell you what kind of client I'm looking for and you tell me if you know anyone who fits that profile. I need to tell you this though, I'm only looking for one or two clients in the next six months. I want to grow slowly so that I can continue to service my current clients."*

Cold Calls

I like cold calls but only to **affinity** groups. Suppose you have worked in the last year with a large number of engineering firms. The affinity group in this case would be other engineering firms. Get a list of other firms who match in size and demographics and make this phone call: *"Herb, this is John with ABC. What I know is that we've worked with several firms like yours in the city helping them to do a, b and c (here, tell them what problems you solve). But, what I don't know is if you are open at all to having some informal dialogue about whether there would be any fit between our companies."*

> Fall seven times.
> Stand up eight.
>
> JAPANESE PROVERB

That's it. No pressure. If he doesn't want to see you, fine. Let it go. You aren't looking to sell or see everyone. You are much too discerning for that. You only want to talk to people who are open. These are the people with whom you share common traits or philosophies. If you belong to a club or an association, this would be an affinity group.

INFORMAL NETWORKS are those circles of influence that you have established over the years. It could be your accountant's clients, your attorney's clients, your barber or hair stylist's clients and your neighbor's friends.

ALLIANT PARTNERS are a misunderstood and severely underutilized vehicle for business growth. In essence, you are asking the question—who else calls on the same people I do? From that list, you will have your potential alliant partners, with whom you can structure deals, arrangements or informal meetings. Drive down the interstate and see how many Shell stations are also McDonald's restaurants—same building, same entrance. They realize the power of alliances. They're after the same customer.

SPEECHES are great if you're in a business where there is information people want. Every civic club is looking for people who can speak in front of a group and bring value in some way. Teleconferencing is another way to do it without having to be there.

ARTICLES you write for newspaper, magazines or trade press are good as well. You can hire a free-lance editor to interview you and write a 500-word article for well under $250. Yes, you do have something to say, if you would allow yourself the chance.

LETTERS are another way to introduce yourself to your prospects or reintroduce yourself to past clients. But have a professional write the letter. Don't be afraid to invest $200 in it. The question throughout this process should be, "What would I invest to generate another $75,000 in income?"

The INTERNET is a helpful tool in lead generation. It's just that most companies don't use it very well for that. On most sites (as of this writing), a brochure is what appears most often. It might be a brochure that moves, dances and java-jumps around the screen, but it's still a brochure. Make sure you have a site that walks people through the kinds of problems you solve in your business? Have them point and click on the most common pains you fix and let them see that you have a solution of value. Then, walk them through step by step to the ultimate goal of getting their name for an email newsletter that you publish educating them more to your process. No selling. No bragging. No self-indulgent, ego-gratifying verbiage. It's about creating an environment that makes it safe for them to see your problem-solving ability and call you.

What About Non-Sales Activity?

Many of us spend some of our day focused on non-sales activity. The same process works. Take any area of your life in which you want to improve and chances are it has a behavioral component to it. If you're a manager and need to stay on the look-out for good people, then you should have a Concerted Market Activity plan to expose you to those people. Maybe you attend five networking groups every month. Maybe you make five calls a month to your current clients asking them if they've seen any good people cross their paths. Whatever the behavior should be, just remember to be "concerted and consistent" with it.

A C T I O N   I T E M

Have a Concerted Market Activity plan because you, and only you, are responsible for your income and the time you invest generating it. If your marketing department is light on leads or if the leads they provide are weak or to the wrong prospect, you must do it yourself. After assessing your inventory of clients and the sources from which you draw them, plan on having at least three streams of market activity. Stick to it as you wind your way from your current income to heights you've never imagined.

Remember, though it should not be created without reading and implementing the exercises in the previous insight. Without Vision and an inspired picture of your future, this CMA calculation won't work.

Inventory of Clients

_____

_____

_____

_____

_____

_____

Three Streams of Market Activity

1. _____

2. _____

3. _____

YOU ONLY HAVE ONE CHANCE AT A CLEAN BEGINNING

OLD THINKING	NEW THINKING
If I can just talk with enough people, the law of numbers will eventually pay me dividends.	My time is my most precious asset. Just talking with more people isn't enough. I must understand the psychology of a masterful beginning when I first start a dialogue with prospects.

In our consulting practice we have companies approach us continuously with a need for help. In 1998, a software company came to us. While most companies struggle with getting enough conversations going, these people were different. They were getting great response from their direct mail program but they couldn't close the sale. The process would drag on and on. Every month the sales cycle would drag on, their cost of sale would go up. Sometimes, their cost of sale was so high, their best move was to **not** make the sale. When their sales process exceeded three months, they actually lost money. They had tried to fix the problem in the eleventh hour by trying to get the prospect to make a decision, but that didn't work either. After some assessment, we found that the problem was occurring much earlier. In truth, it was happening at the first contact.

So we made a micro change in their approach to that first call. In the old approach, when a prospect called in, they would ask the prospect three questions:

- *What kind of system do you currently have?*
- *How many users are on that system?*
- *Who is the decision-maker?*

The first two questions were OK—it was information they had to have eventually, but didn't need up front. The last question, about the decision-maker, was worthless. Why would you ask a question the answer to which you know is probably a lie? In fact, many times the prospect didn't have a clue regarding the decision process within their own company.

Here is what we coached them to ask and think:

- *I'm curious—what was there in the ad you saw that prompted you to make this call?*
- *What impact does that condition (from the first question) have on your business?*
- *What role do you play in all of this?*

The results were astounding. Almost immediately, they had deeper conversations with their prospects. They reduced the sales process time by twenty-five percent. They hiked their closing rate from twenty percent of quotations to forty-five percent. And over the course of the year— spread out over twelve salespeople—they reduced their hours spent quoting by 2,000 hours. By asking three different questions—that took no more time to ask than their prior questions—they changed the entire framework of the sales process.

How Do You Start Dialogue?

There are probably only a few ways in which you begin dialogue with prospects. The software company's start happened to be an incoming call. It could be a bounce back lead card where the prospect asks for more information. It could be that you ran into someone at an informal gathering. It could be you're making a cold call or getting a referral.

Whatever it is, have a dialogue builder for each venue.

You have only one chance to build your position. Are you positioned as a needy, begging seller doing anything possible to close a deal? Or, are you a savvy problem solver with so much business in your pipeline that, although you are looking to help your prospect, you won't be able to spend much time if it isn't a "fit?" I hope you're the second. The beginning is where the subtle points of control get set. It's where the relationship gets started as an adult-to-adult dialogue where truth can be exchanged. If you've ever had a prospect lie to you or mislead you, it resulted from a weak beginning.

> What is easy and obvious is never valued; and even what is difficult, if we come to the knowledge of it without difficulty, and without any stretch of thought, is but little regarded.
>
> *DAVID HUME*
> *A Treatise of Human Nature*

Here is the proper attitude to have as you move through the marketplace and begin a dialogue with potential buyers:

> *I will talk to as many people as I can to help them determine if they have a problem I can solve. But when they are problem-free or in denial about the problem and its seriousness, I will move on.*

That attitude will help as you begin to position yourself in the first dialogue. For example, suppose you get a lead and now you're calling the person back. Let's just say that a few weeks have gone by since your prospect filled out the card. Here is the conversation:

> *John, let me tell you what has happened. You apparently sent in a card asking for more information about the Squicket 5000. Here's my problem. I don't know if I can help or, if you've solved the problem. Can I ask you a question? What prompted you to send the request in to us?*

How many calls would you have to take, using that script, to get invited in to see five people? Probably not 100. Why? Because you've changed the entire perspective of the cold call. You're not begging them to buy from you. Instead, you are filtering and screening out the people who will waste your time. In fact, you're even telling them up front that there may be nothing you can do for them. The fact is you only want five, so even if they say yes to an appointment, you aren't going until you know they're worth your time. Try it 100 times and hit our website **www. caskeytraining.com**. Let us know how you did.

Isn't that approach better than the old way?

> *John, this is Bill of Squicket Enterprises. We're so damn happy you sent in this bounce back card that we'll do everything we can to get you to buy this from us. I'm going to send you our 900 page catalog that*

*you can read over the holidays and I'll call you back
in a week to take your order.*

Take that approach and you'll waste the next six weeks trying to get them to call you back. Do it differently. As you master the beginning of the process, the rest gets easy. Selling becomes fun and the reward, which awaits you at the end of each process, is larger.

A C T I O N   I T E M

Use these words the next time you begin the sales process:

> *Tom, thanks for having me out. What I'd like to do is ask you some things about your company and some of the challenges you have. I'd like you to feel free to ask me about what we do. At the end of today we can decide if there is any reason to talk further. If there is, we can talk about what happens next. If there's not, that's fine—we can decide to do nothing.*

TOO MUCH ENTHUSIASM COSTS YOU MONEY

OLD THINKING	NEW THINKING
Enthusiasm is contagious. If I can get someone to like me with enthusiasm, I will make the sale.	Enthusiasm is frightening to others. It is dangerous and will cause people to lean away, rather than toward you.

Somewhere along the line, we were misinformed—not intentionally, but repeatedly. Whether trainers, public speakers, pastors, teachers or parents did it to us, I don't know. We have been told for ages that enthusiasm sells. We've been told to have a big smile, a loud voice, an enthusiastic nature and we will attract people to us in droves. We've been coached by our managers to act happy, be magnetic, charming, charismatic and enthusiastic.

The Myth Is Exposed

Overt enthusiasm does not sell. It frightens. It does so because it makes us cautious of the hidden motives of the enthusiasm. Sometimes when we're the buyer, on the other end of the sales process, that little inner voice which guides our actions whispers to us, "Why is this sales rep so damned enthusiastic? Better watch out. It looks suspicious." And it is suspicious

In my business, I have worked with people at both ends of the income spectrum—from the $20,000 entry-level person to the $2 million CEO. Can I let you in on a secret that I wouldn't have suspected when I entered this business ten years ago?

> The more you lean on someone else, the leaner become your chances of success.
>
> *PROVERB*

The secret is this. High income does not follow high enthusiasm. The opposite is true. The less overtly enthusiastic a seller is about his product, the more he will sell. And the more he sells, the more money he makes. The reason he will earn more is that he has conviction in his ability to solve problems, rather than in his zeal to sell a product. This new rule of thought will give you the confidence to believe in market abundance—rather than just in the features and benefits of your product. In my training, I have a rule that I tell people on the first day of training. I tell them it goes against most of what they've heard in the old school. The rule is this:

R U L E

Enthusiasm makes people like you.
Solving their problems makes them buy from you.

Suppose you went in to the doctor's office with a pain in your chest. You just started noticing it a few days ago and it seemed to be getting a little worse each day. Rather than take any chances with your heart, you decided to make an appointment. When you get there, the doc enters. "What seems to be the problem?" he asks.

After you tell him in detail what is happening, he jumps up out of his chair and starts smiling ear to ear. He says "Man, am I glad you came in today. I am so excited for you, you won't believe it. About three weeks ago, I bought a new, state-of-the-art scalpel that has some features and benefits you won't believe. It has a platinum head, which makes the incision painless. It has a rubber grommet handle that helps it stay steady in my hand. And one more thing—we have a brand new lighting system in the operating room that is shadowless and provides 125% more light on the table. I think this is going to be great! Let's go ahead and cut you open and find out what's in there!"

> By being detached, you have a clearer view inside people's humanity; you soon understand what people want. Understanding what people want is a way of getting very rich very quickly.
>
> *STUART WILDE*
> *The Infinite Self*

Wouldn't you be a little suspect of that doctor's zeal to fix the problem? Wouldn't you have some suspicion about why he's so quick to cut? Wouldn't you wonder why he is so enthusiastic—when you're sitting there in pain and worried sick? I would. I think you would, too. Actually, you'd probably end the appointment abruptly and run out of the office before he grabbed the scalpel. His enthusiasm and zeal are misplaced—and frightening.

So why is selling any different? It isn't. You are the doctor. You have the solution to your prospect's problem. You have the medicine to help him get well, even if you can't actually treat him. You possess the expertise and wisdom to solve virtually all of the problems in your area of concern—so why would enthusiasm ever enter in to it? So, be like a good doctor. Never be enthusiastic. It scares people.

Rather, let them see your concern. Let them see your worry. Let them know you can sense a little of the discomfort they must be going through. You don't have to put them on the couch and do therapy— I've seen people try that and it can be ugly. Never be more enthusiastic about selling than the prospect is about solving

> Be modest. It is the kind of pride least likely to offend.
>
> *LEO SHESTOV*
> *All Things are Possible*

their problem. When you are, you start to lean on them and toward them. And when you lean on them, you risk pushing them out the window. Then you lose the prospect forever.

Remedy

It's OK to smile—to have a nice manner about you. It's OK to call someone by their first name even though you don't know them. But don't go overboard on the rapport. Don't do the move where you use their first name five times in the first sentence. That's phony and manipulative and they see it. Be real. Be interested. Be in the present moment with your potential client—not thinking about how you're going to spend the commission money, or how much of a hero you'll be by landing the account, but by being right there with your prospect in his pain.

Honoring the Insight—What Happens When They Call You on It?

When I tell my clients to lose the enthusiasm, they get very nervous. It's almost as if I'm transgressing the scriptures, where somewhere it is written, "be enthusiastic!" The fear is that your prospect is going to see you aren't as excited as the other five people who were in there selling to him, and somehow you're going to get "caught." Here's a story of a client who did.

"Get Out of My Office!"

I have a client, John, who earns over $150,000 a year selling telecommunications equipment. He is a very good salesperson. John follows our method meticulously. He is exquisite at orchestrating the sales process, which sometimes can go on for months in his business. The other day he called and said, "Bill, I had a prospect nearly throw me out of his office because he said he didn't feel like I was enthusiastic enough—he didn't feel like I wanted the business bad enough."

What he was bringing up is something we hear all the time. When the salesperson enters the process without outward enthusiasm, it sometimes makes the prospect uncomfortable. It isn't something the prospect is used to seeing.

> He who truly knows,
> has no occasion to shout.
>
> *LEONARDO DA VINCI*

"What did you tell him?" I asked.

John's response:

> *Look sir. I understand your concern. I have a lot of things going on right now. I'm working with many prospects trying to help them solve their telecom problems. My enthusiasm and energy peak when we both decide it's a fit to work together. If I'm too enthusiastic up front about my product, then you don't get a chance to tell me your problems. And if I don't know your problems, how in the world can I ever help you fix them? So I've trained myself to be more interested in solving your problems than in getting hyped up about my product. However, if you're looking for someone who is purely enthusiastic, then perhaps I'm not your guy.*

John's a good student. He didn't get defensive. Nor did he get enthusiastic. After explaining the issues, the prospect not only wanted him to stay, but ended up revealing much deeper issues than he had before—or than he had revealed to others. He told John more about the decision process, more about the competition that had already been in, and more about the core problems they were trying to avoid and the vision they were trying to achieve. Why? Because John had not only been unenthusiastic, but had shared with the prospect his full intent and philosophy. And it was a philosophy the prospect couldn't argue with.

> Too much zeal offends,
> where indirection works.
>
> *EURIPEDES*
> Orestes

When you practice this insight, you may get called on it. When you do, honor your prospect's concern and immediately reveal your philosophy. Everything will be OK. Your prospect will get their problem solved. You'll go to the bank.

As Saturday Night Live's former star Dana Carvey (a.k.a. George Bush) might say "From now on—enthusiasm—not gonna do it."

A C T I O N   I T E M

On your next sales call, sit back and relax. Don't be too excited. Have conviction, but not excitement. Stay humble about you and your product. Practice the principle of "problem first, enthusiasm second."

SELLING IS HALF INTELLECT AND HALF EMOTION

OLD THINKING	NEW THINKING
My prospect wants facts, figures, features, data and proof that my solution is the best.	Yes, facts and features are important, but my prospect's emotions are more powerful than any proof I can give him.

Most selling systems are based on a hopelessly outdated premise—that selling is intellectual. Those methods are based on an illusion: if you tell enough features and benefits, your prospects will magically come to the conclusion that their previous decisions were wrong and that to right those wrongs they must take money out of their pocket and give it to you. Do you really think that's smart?

Most selling processes hide the fact that selling is a rich combination of both intellect and pure emotion. Sure, there is some intellectual justification the further into the process one gets—but at the outset, you must know how emotions work so you can open up your prospect. Get him to tell you about his problems.

The prospect has his ego involved from the start as you begin to talk. Ego is pure emotion. And most of the time, it's rooted in fear. That fear comes in several different areas—fear that you will do something to hurt him (psychologically), fear that you will expose his previous wrongs, fear that he will make the wrong decision and fear that by opening up to you, you will destroy his pride and dignity. The list goes on and on. And that list is longer if you approach him intellectually. Every pain your prospect has impacts him at an emotional level. It is impossible to solve an emotional problem intellectually.

> Many a man would rather you heard his story than grant his request.
>
> LORD CHESTERFIELD

The part most salespeople miss is how emotional the initial part of the sales process is. That's why you must strive to make the prospect OK right up front. Adding this little step to your process will set you apart and make you more money.

You must find yourself saying things like:

- *I don't know if this will help you.*
- *I don't know if you have any interest in talking about this (not, I don't know if you have any interest in buying this).*
- *I don't know this . . .*
- *I don't know that . . .*
- *I'm not sure if I even belong here.*

The less you know, the safer he will feel about sharing with you what he knows—which is usually pure emotion.

Make it safe for him to open up and talk with you. It's only if he's revealing his compelling reasons to you that he will connect your solution with his problem. But if you can't even get him to open up and be revealing, then you won't go much further. Be safe. Be non-threatening.

People buy for two core reasons:

1. To eliminate a current or impending problem (pain).
2. To realize some kind of new opportunity or gain (pleasure).

They can both be very compelling reasons and, as often is the case, in a business-to-business setting they are intricately linked. But to think that a person buys from you because of your beautiful marketing brochure or easy-to-use web site is to ignore the psychology and natural forces of self-interest.

When you evoke one or both of these elements—pain or pleasure—from your prospect, you are gathering crucial information in your decision process about whether you want to continue to work with him. And it's critical for your prospect to begin to understand the emotional buying reasons, which he has. You are helping him to make a decision by the questions you ask and the way you ask them.

Pain

Pain has nothing to do with needs. And don't be fooled into thinking that pain has anything to do with the features of your product. The best kind of pain the prospect can be in, as far as you're concerned, revolves around the problems that exist because you aren't a part of his life. In order to find out what pain compels that prospect, you must make it OK for his ego to tell you. The ego will not want to admit any shortcomings until it senses there is no danger. So you must be very careful up front, and make it safe for him to admit these challenges. When you get him to reveal these issues or these prevailing conditions which exist because of your absence, you're moving forward. His revelation of pain is pure emotion. (More on Pain in Insight 23).

Unexploited Opportunity

While the pain of his current reality is often at or near the surface, unexploited or undiscovered opportunity is sub-conscious. The trick to finding this out and bringing it to the surface is, again, ego removal. First, you must make a conscious effort to remove your ego from the game. In other words (as part of the Principle of Detachment, Insight 4) you must really not care whether you get the business. Instead, only care whether or not you help him identify his hidden opportunity. Then, you must nurture his ego as well. Tell him this. "I work with other companies and help them exploit opportunities they didn't even know about, but I'm not sure I can help you."

> We are more easily persuaded, in general, by the reasons we ourselves discover, than by those which are given to us by others.
>
> *BLAISE PASCAL*

Pain is about solving problems today and in the future.

Unexploited opportunity is about your client achieving a future gain.

Can you put your need for the sale aside long enough to determine what your prospect's self-interest is? It takes a bit of ego-removal medicine to do that. There is no way you'll ever get close to understanding their self-interest if you are in hard-sell mode. You'll run up against gates of resistance at each step in the sales process.

Here are two role-plays to help you see what happens when you can capture his self-interests instead of being full of your own ego.

Old Dog / Traditional Salesperson

Prospect: I'm thinking about changing suppliers in my warehousing software. They tell me you can do a good job. Tell me a little about your company and your product.

Seller: I'd be happy to. We've been in business for over seventy-five years and are the largest software supplier in a five-state area. We have worked with many similar companies and have really changed the way they do business. In fact, we were written up recently in National Software News and our business is great.

Prospect: How much is your system?

Seller: Well, it depends on what you want.

Prospect: I want something to handle fifty-six seats and five LANS.

Seller: We did one down the road, which was close to that—about $50,000.

Prospect: $50,000!! I don't have that kind of money.

Seller: Well, we could do a lease deal where you could pay for it over time . . .

On and on the seller goes, working on the wrong problem. He got himself in trouble early with his approach and his inability to gain control of the situation. He ended up working on the price problem, when in reality, it had nothing to do with price—and everything to do with belief. He never got to the prospect's emotional issue. He was too enthusiastic about his company, his product and the article.

Here's another one:

Old Dog / New Breed of Salesperson

Prospect:	I'm thinking about changing suppliers in my warehousing software. They tell me you can do a good job. Tell me a little about your company and your product.
Seller:	I'd be happy to—one problem though—I must tell you right up front that I'm not sure we can help you. We've worked with a lot of companies like yours, but everyone is so different. Let's do this. Is it OK if I ask you some questions about the problem you're trying to solve? Then you ask me some about how we've helped other people in similar situations. Then we can decide what our next steps might be—if any. My intent here is to determine if there would be any reason to talk further.
Prospect:	That's fine.
Seller:	Usually we find that people are interested in this type of software for three reasons. One, either they have a current problem they are trying to solve; two, a future problem which is impending; or three, they are looking to expand into new areas—perhaps looking to take advantage of a market opportunity.
Prospect:	Well, it's really the first. We're getting bogged down in details. Our current system doesn't lend itself to the way we're doing business and I need a solution pretty quickly.
Seller:	When you say "quickly" what do you mean? Why so quickly?
Prospect:	Well, we just took on a new account and it begins in three months. If we drop the ball on these guys, some heads are going to roll. This will be a $500,000 account, our largest one ever.

Do you see the difference between the two scenarios? Did you see how much more open the prospect was in the second scenario? If the prospect would have said it wasn't a current problem—that it, instead, had to do with future growth—then the seller could have asked about the company vision, the dreams he had for his department and how he saw the world in three to five years.

But it wasn't appropriate in this context.

R U L E

Evoke first and educate second.

Your sole purpose on any first call should be to find out what the conditions are which caused the prospective client to invite you in or agree to see you. There is always something. People don't do things without a reason. In the second scenario, the seller was able to create the right environment and take control of the process. He didn't do it with overt, angry control—rather, he was gentle, assertive, nurturing and made the prospect feel good about sharing his problem This set him apart from the first seller. Who would your clients prefer to do business with?

> The heart has reasons that reason does not know.
>
> **BLAISE PASCAL**

Call It Pain or Call It Pleasure, It's Really Self-Interest

Change is tough, yes. But change is less difficult if your prospect sees that change is in his best interest. The thing that most salespeople can't figure out is how to help the prospect see that change is in their interest. We go to product training school and get injected with great product knowledge, but when we talk about those features and benefits with our prospect, it leaves them frigid.

Most of the time, we erroneously try to force change by the worn-out art of persuasion—in other words, by force. When you do that, you'll actually force your prospect away from you. You click into the prospect's ego and their ego responds by saying "no thanks."

A much stronger tactic is to be with that prospect emotionally. Be inside their mind and brain. Find out what they want in life and if your solution helps them get there, you'll move forward. If the connection is too much of a stretch, then you won't. But that's OK. You can move on at any time to pursue people who you can help.

The high-income producers and the people who make selling look easy are those who are artful in helping the prospect see that change is in their self-interest. But never do they tell them that outright. Rather, the sales professional comes to the table being OK with wherever the prospect is on the continuum of pain. And slightly, ever so slightly, moving them back and forth, until the proper moment comes when you advance the sale.

A C T I O N   I T E M

What problem do you solve for your clients in your business? What kind of undiscovered opportunity are you going to help them with? Write a paragraph on each of those two questions and share it with others in your business. If you run up against an old thinker— one who tells you not to worry about that, but to keep on vomiting features and benefits, move away quickly from that energy. You don't want that rubbing off on you. Ask someone else.

KNOW HOW AND WHY PEOPLE TAKE ACTION

OLD THINKING	NEW THINKING
People buy a product to fill a need.	People go through a process when they make decisions. I must understand what this process is and act accordingly.

It's amazing to me how many business and salespeople don't have a clue how to get someone to change from inaction to action. In other words, how to get them from their current way of doing things to your way of doing or seeing things. Can you imagine not understanding how to do the exact activity that puts money in your pocket?

It is your role as a sales professional to understand how and why people make the decisions they make. It's rooted deep in behavioral psychology and as you might have guessed, we're going to address it. Baltasar Gracian said, "Many people spend time analyzing the properties of animals or herbs; how much more important it would be to study those properties of people, with whom we must live or die?"

People go through stages when making purchasing decisions. Whether they're buying a product or service, new or old, one-time sale or ongoing relationship, these stages are unconscious. Here are the five stages they go through:

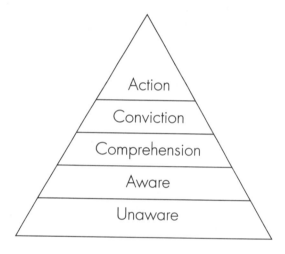

FIGURE 1

Let's discuss your role in moving someone through these steps.

Unaware to Aware

The first thing you must do is take someone from point A to point B. If they are unaware of you as a company or as a person, your first job is to build awareness. If they are aware of you at one level of problem-solving, but not at other levels, then you still have a task ahead of you. Marketing is a way to make people aware of you, but not the only way. Even a cold call can do that. Understand that this is only one part of the process, but an important one.

Awareness to Comprehension

Once they are aware of you, they should next comprehend both what you do and how that could help them. In other words, they need to know, at an intellectual level, what problem you will solve for them. They must comprehend what problems they have, and understand that they're serious enough to require action. You take people there by asking them questions like—why are you interested in this? What is the future vision if you get this problem fixed?

Comprehension to Conviction

This is where emotion comes in to play. Not only must they believe they have a problem—it's imperative they acknowledge that it must be solved. Moreover, they must have conviction that you, and only you, can solve that problem. This is where your value must be translated. You will be nurturing but tough in this stage of the process. They have to be convinced that they have a problem worth solving, and you have a solution worth investing in. You must ask questions like: Who else have you looked at to help you solve this? What did they say? Why didn't you buy from them? What happens if you decide not to get this fixed?

Conviction to Action

This is really quite easy if you've done the other steps. You must develop a process, which helps them go from conviction to action very carefully. When someone gets ready to take action, they often get scared at the last minute. That's why so many deals fall apart at the end. It had nothing to do with your fantastic presentation. Your prospect got scared and you made it easier for him to back out than to get his problem solved. If you're having trouble moving people from conviction to action, you've either moved them through the process too quickly or have completely skipped a step. You help them by laying out the process like we did in Insight 3.

Danger in Vaulting

Vaulting is what amateur salespeople do. Because they are ignoring the buyer's process, they attempt to move him through their process too quickly or skip steps. Most salespeople skip the comprehension step and move straight from awareness to action. The result? The prospect gets scared and bows out or shops around. You may eventually get the deal, but it will take you much longer—and you'll get it at a lower margin.

A C T I O N   I T E M

Take four deals you are currently working on and plot where you think you are on this model.

Prospect _____

| Unawareness | Awareness | Comprehension | Conviction | Action |

Prospect _____

| Unawareness | Awareness | Comprehension | Conviction | Action |

Prospect _____

| Unawareness | Awareness | Comprehension | Conviction | Action |

Prospect _____

| Unawareness | Awareness | Comprehension | Conviction | Action |

You're Always in Danger of Sinking into the Commodity Dungeon

OLD THINKING	NEW THINKING
My outstanding features and benefits will be clear enough to justify my price.	My approach and selling method—not my features and benefits—propels me out of the commodity dungeon.

It's a place you don't want to end up. The surroundings are bad, the environment is ugly and it causes you to be exceedingly weak in the sales process. You know what I'm talking about—it's the commodity dungeon.

The commodity dungeon is an easy place to fall into and a hard place to get out of. You end up there when the prospect perceives your product, your service or your entire offering as just one of many commodities they could buy. It's the attitude, "You've seen one, you've seen them all."

Now keep this in mind—because the prospect wants approval every bit as much as you do, he is probably not going to tell you that he perceives your product as a commodity. The meeting where he admits you're just like everyone else is one you're not invited to—where he and his decision-making team are sizing up the alternatives and the options. That's when you become a commodity.

What's remarkable to me is the number of companies who really do bring extra, incremental value and are quite easily differentiated from their competitors—yet who end up in the commodity dungeon because their salespeople can't figure out a way to extract themselves from it. Why? Because they haven't created a philosophy to translate that value to the customer.

How do you end up in the commodity dungeon? The following list will give you a clue:

External Pressure from Prospects

It probably makes you ill to think about all the times you've been asked to give a quote only to be compared to another competitor who didn't bring as much value as you did. But the prospect looked at one thing and one thing only—price. What's worse is that pressure forces you to believe what your prospect believes—that it's all about price—thereby forcing you back to the dungeon. It's true that if you hear something enough times, you start believing it.

Cultural Sensitivity to Price

When you open the newspaper on Sunday morning what do you see? Over 5,000 ads touting "low prices," "best prices in town," "guaranteed low prices," and "beat our prices and we'll give you 5% off." So is it any wonder that when a culture so predisposed to price buys a business-to-business product, price is an early and major contributor to the decision-making process?

Clutter in the Market

If you're not a low-price provider, but you have low-price competitors, they'll probably force the price issue as their only differential advantage. Low-price providers are taught to say, "Really, both units are equal—it's just a matter of what you want to pay."

The above three clues really come at you from the outside and you have little control over any of them. But you do have control over the fourth one.

Your Approach to Your Prospect and the Ensuing Sales Process

You are the only one who can let your process default to the commodity dungeon. One of the greatest sayings of all time is, "You can't control how people treat you, but you can control your reaction to how people treat you." So let's work on things you can control; namely, your approach to the prospect.

The following model illustrates what happens when a prospect asks the traditional, old-breed salesperson, "Why should I buy from you?" We've selected the entries on each line of the model to illustrate how most people really sell. These are the top five statements salespeople make when asked that question. We've set this out in columns so that you can get a clear picture about what happens.

So what do you suppose happens when every person in the process looks alike? Do they buy from the best-looking person? Do they buy from the person with the cleanest web site? Or do they buy on price? More often than not, when everyone looks and sounds alike, they will buy on price. Is that what you want?

By the way, the answer to the question "Why should I buy from you?" is always:

> *You know, that's a good question. I'm not so sure there is a reason for you to buy from us. In fact, the only*

You Say	Competitor #1 Says	Competitor #2 Says
Competitive prices	Competitive prices	Competitive prices
Great reputation	Great reputation	Great reputation
Our customers love us	Our customers love us	Our customers love us
We have excellent quality	We have excellent quality	We have excellent quality
We've been around a long time	We've been around a long time	We've been around a long time

FIGURE 2

reason I can think of is that we would solve a problem better or differently than one of our competitors. Would you mind sharing some of the challenges around here with me and let's see if there's a compelling reason for you to work with us.

That starts to get you out of the commodity dungeon.

R U L E
_____

Your income expands in proportion to how well you remove yourself from the commodity dungeon.

R U L E
_____

The way you decommoditize your offering is to identify the prospect's proprietary pain—which no one else knows or can solve.

A STORY TO ILLUSTRATE

This story supposedly happened in the 70s in Memphis, Tennessee. I wasn't there and can't vouch for the absolute honesty of the story, but it sounds feasible and I've heard it in different variations before.

Fred Smith, the CEO of Federal Express, was approached by a local employment staffing service and asked what kinds of problems he was having in growing his shipping airline.

Smith apparently said that one of his biggest concerns in staffing was never having the right number of people on staff at night when the planes came in. He wasn't sure how many packages to staff up for. On some nights he'd be paying people to sit around and twiddle their thumbs and on other nights they'd be so overwhelmed by the quantity of packages that some wouldn't get shipped. The staffing rep asked him how much he thought that problem was cost-ing Federal Express. Smith apparently replied, "Millions of dollars. Hundreds of thousands of dollars now, but millions of dollars in the future."

> Man does not sell commodities. He sells himself and feels himself to be a commodity.
>
> *ERICH FROMM*
> *Escape from Freedom*

So the staffing rep went back, thought about the problem, and came back with a solution. Fred bought the solution and the staffing rep had a new client—a big one.

Before I continue the story, here's my question: Did Fred Smith worry about the hourly rate of the employees at that point? Did he fret over what margin the temporary service was making on his account? Probably not. It doesn't mean he wasn't conscious of the cost, but he saw the big picture and understood the value the solution could bring Federal Express. He was in no position to beat the rep down on price. The rep provided such a fabulous solution, saving the company hundreds of thousands—if not millions—of dollars, that Smith didn't care what he spent per hour to get that done.

Fast-forward a couple of years. At some point Mr. Smith was not able to handle the details of the business and moved on to bigger and better things—creating the vision for the company. In turn, he delegated a lot of his staffing decisions to his VP of Operations, who, incidentally, was not there at the beginning when the original staffing problem was solved.

One day the staffing rep got a call from the Federal Express VP of Operations who said, "You've got to come in here quick, we've got a pricing problem. We're going to put this thing out to bid with five other staffing agencies." After the staffing rep swallowed hard, got in his car and drove there, he realized what had happened.

His product had become a commodity. Why? Because there was no longer a big picture problem tied to the solution. Plus, he didn't have a good relationship with the VP of Operations, so he wasn't even able to find out what his problems were and create solutions for them.

R U L E

When the original problem gets solved, you must look for other problems to solve with your current clients.

When you don't follow the above rule, the conversation and focus will end up back on price. All of your competitors are in there chipping away at you. They have no clue about the problem and solution mentality.

Help the prospect identify the problem. Help frame the problem in the biggest picture solution you can (i.e. even Fred Smith wasn't looking to solve a staffing problem—he wanted to solve a financial and business one). Give people a solution to it and watch the money roll in.

FedEx ended up staying with our friend's staffing service. However, the incident caused him "margin pain." A 20% discount in price led to a 50% decrease in margin. As it ended up, the failure of the staffing company to have a problem-solving relationship with the client cost them hundreds of thousands of dollars.

If you're selling on features, benefits and your good looks, and disregard the problem your prospect is trying to solve by purchasing your product, then you'll end up back in the smelly pits of the commodity dungeon every day.

One final thought. Many people plead with us to accept that their product is a commodity and there's absolutely nothing they can do to change that except lower the price. That's a wimpy way to look at it and only in certain industries—probably less than one percent—is your product really a commodity.

A C T I O N   I T E M

Try this. Spend the next two weeks writing, journalling and contemplating on what other non-commodity aspects there are to your product. Then make that the focus of your conversation around the prospect's problems.

THIS IS THE "HALF-TIME GUT CHECK"

If you were in one of my workshops this would be the point where I would call a time-out. I do that because reflection time is a key ingredient in learning. You will remember more when you stop occasionally, close your eyes—unless you're driving—and contemplate the philosophies. Consequently, it's a time to look back and review what you've learned. To do this, I suggest that you review any notes you've made, and any rules you have set in your journal, on page 181. How are you doing?

HIGH INTENT YIELDS HIGH RESULTS

OLD THINKING	NEW THINKING
My intent is to get the prospect to say yes and buy from me.	My intent is to help my prospect discover, reveal and solve the problems he has, and in doing so determine if I can help him.

In life, you accept responsibility for what appears in your world. If you look around and find yourself in a place of lack and scarcity and don't have the things that provide you with enrichment, then you must look at your intent in business. I say "business" because, for most of us, business is the channel that provides income. So if we're going to change our income, we must look at the source. What is your intent in business?

Is your intent to make quota? Is it to win the monthly contest? Is it to get your customer to buy now, even though it may be in his best interest to wait three months?

> In confidence and quietness shall be your strength.
>
> *ISAIAH 30:15. KJV*

Intent causes an effect. If your intent is to sell your prospect no matter what, that intent will come across to the prospect. And what do you suppose he'll do? You guessed it. He'll stall, lie, object, delay, and do everything else that his internal voices are screaming at him to do. Just as you have an intuition which protects you, so does he.

When his intuition is screaming, "Watch out! Danger! You're about to be sold!" you can't expect to sell him. If you don't like your results in sales or in your income, then check out your intent.

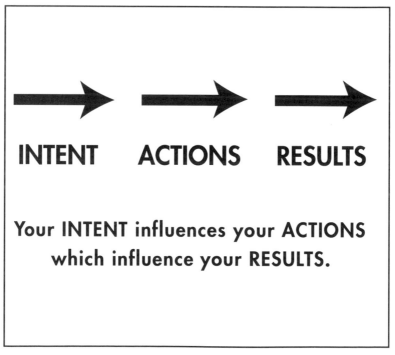

INTENT   **ACTIONS**   **RESULTS**

Your INTENT influences your ACTIONS which influence your RESULTS.

FIGURE 3

What should your intent be? Here's one that I've found can give you tremendous power, both from an inner game standpoint and in the marketplace as well.

> *Your intent should be to help the prospect*
> *identify, reveal and fix his problem, even if*
> *he decides not to use you to get it fixed.*

Yes, that's right—even if he uses someone else. When that is your intent, and you're unattached to the outcome, think of the strength you possess. What you are saying is that you're OK regardless of what he does. You come from a place of unconditional support—and how often do you get unconditional support anywhere in life? Conversely, when you come at the prospect in the traditional manner, where you love him only if he buys from you—conditional support—you weaken your position.

Don't you think your new intent will empower you both to arrive at the best conclusion? When that's your intent, watch what happens to your techniques. They'll come from the heart. They will come easier and you'll experience less fear—all because the intent is sound and in both of your best interests. But you'll also be much stronger in managing your process. Remember, selling is a process, not an art form. And any kind of power you can derive from your heart—the power of intent—will be of extreme value to you in moving through the process.

> How successful you are in sales and business is dependent upon how well you translate your value to your customer. With the right intent, you raise your odds of success.
>
> **BILL CASKEY**

Steve, a print broker who attends our regular workshops, has built his business on the attitude of intent. He knows something his competitors haven't yet figured out. People are attracted to him not because of the phenomenal printing plants he represents, nor his pricing, which often can be higher. But he wins business because he tells his prospects right up front,

> *My whole intent of this first call is to ask you some questions so that we can determine together whether there is a fit between us. After fifteen years in this business, and thousands of clients—I realize that our suppliers are not perfect for everyone. So my intent is to help you get your problem solved—whether you use me or not.*

He earns well in excess of $250,000 a year, and will tell you that his income has tripled since he adopted the correct intent and reveals it to his prospect.

But he's not perfect. He'll also tell you that when business is soft he has to work extra hard on his inner game so he doesn't fall back into old thinking. Fortunately, when he's practicing the new rule of right intent, business is attracted to him.

Conclusion/Action Step

To avoid being average, stay away from the wrong intent. Begin looking for ways to solve the problems of your prospect, not just to sell him something that's not directed to his specific problems.

A C T I O N   I T E M

Take a deal that you are working on right now. Perhaps it just began, or maybe it's in the latter phases.
Pick one that is somewhat stalled. Go back mentally to
the last couple of meetings and decide what your true
intent has been. Has it been to sell him a product? Has
it been to get the deal done? And, what did you tell him
your intent was? Sometimes, our intent can be pure, but
if we don't tell the prospect exactly what it is, we lose
the power of it. To that, some would say "well, if your
intent is pure, you shouldn't have to tell him what it is."
I disagree. Sometimes you just have to tell people what
you're up to.

If you have a deal that is stalled, set up a meeting
with that prospect and reveal to him your "high intent"
(to help him identify and solve a problem). Do so with
the purpose of either ending the process (it might be
over anyway) or starting over—correctly.

KEEP THEM OK AND GO TO THE BANK

OLD THINKING	NEW THINKING
I am here to sell. I'm too busy to worry about how my prospect is "feeling."	Every one of us is striving for psychological OKness. My prospect is no different. When I keep him feeling safe, he will be more open and allow me to solve the real problem.

Everyone wants to be right. The proverb says, "Most people would rather be right than rich." We all have gigantic egos, which scream at us when someone gives us information that conflicts with our current belief. So chances are, if you're in front of a potential client attempting to affect change or motivate him to do something different, you'll bump up against resistance. In most cases, the resistance is caused by him not being OK with your pressure to change him. When people get not OK due to external pressure, they will defend their previous decisions—vehemently.

Consequently, you must be meticulous about keeping your prospect OK throughout the sales process. There are many ways to do this, one is to acknowledge the intelligence of past decisions he has made—or to acknowledge that current conditions may not be that bad or worth fixing. If he has pain—he probably does or you wouldn't be there—he will make sure you know it.

> Ninety percent of what you've learned about selling is wrong. It neutralizes your power; it renders you helpless in the process; it sabotages your income.
>
> *BILL CASKEY*

Dr. Thomas Harris, in his 1969 classic book *I'm OK, You're OK*, says the following:

> *As a child attempts to make sense of himself, he figures out his perceived position in the world—I'm not OK and you're OK. It is permanently recorded and will influence everything he does. Because it is a decision, it can be changed by a new decision, but not until it is understood.*

How does the child come to that conclusion? Harris continues:

> *. . . at birth, the little individual is pushed out into a state of catastrophic contrast in which he is exposed to foreign extremes of cold, roughness, pressure, noise, nonsupport, brightness, separateness and abandonment.*

Soon after, feelings of inferiority begin in our lives. We manage to cope as adults on a daily basis. However, when situations arise that make us not OK, we revert back to those early childhood days of inferiority. When we begin to feel those feelings of abandonment, separateness, or a threat to our survival, we take steps to change our world. In business, we experience those feelings everyday. Thankfully, we know that they aren't life-threatening, yet they still affect us. And guess what? They affect our prospect as well.

There are two primary scenarios that cause us discomfort: 1) external pressure that we don't know how to handle, and 2) coming to terms with previous decisions that, in retrospect, are wrong.

External Pressures

By external pressure, I mean "salesperson pressure." When we arrive at the prospect's doorstep, he will immediately drop into a not OK position. He knows what you're there to do. And you know what your manager or director wants from you. You're not OK because you need the sale—he's not OK because he is working on protecting his ego from attack. When you have two not OK people doing battle you have the markings for several things: games being played in the sales process, lying to each other, and a general mistrust of each other, which yields a dishonest process.

> We spend our time searching for security and hate it when we get it.
>
> *JOHN STEINBECK*
> *America and Americans*

What's worse is that you'll never see it. He'll never acknowledge that you made him feel not OK. So you will end up working on a price problem or a decision problem, when, in truth, that wasn't the real problem. The real problem happened earlier when you interrupted him three times in mid-sentence or when your overt enthusiasm left him cold. It takes time to get people OK—to the point where they are willing to tell you their problems. It takes seconds to make them not OK and wanting to get rid of you.

Previous Decisions

Most of the time, as a sales professional, you are looking to enact change in your prospect's action or attitudes. That typically means that we must get them to change from a previous decision that didn't involve us. When you come at someone too aggressively up front, trying to get them to change or try something new, you will encounter resistance. Tread carefully. That's why I encourage all salespeople to tell the prospect up front: *"I don't know if I can help."* It is one of the easiest ways to get your prospect comfortable in admitting any previous errors in decisions. Your role here is to get the prospect to admit things to you (his problems) that he wouldn't ordinarily admit. To do that, you need to be 50% shrink and 50% friend and 0% seller.

> The better we feel about ourselves, the fewer times we have to knock somebody else down to feel tall.
>
> *ODETTA*

By you keeping him OK up front, you will get more information and he won't have to defend past decisions.

What will people do when they are not OK?

Here's a brief list:

- They will lie to you.
- They will hold back information from you that you could use to help them solve their problem.
- They will get rid of you (physically and psychologically).
- They will buy less from you than they could or should have.
- They will not refer you to other people who need what you have.
- They will make implementation of your solution very difficult.

The list could go on forever. The bottom line is that it isn't good for you when they get not OK.

The selling game is played in inches. One very small move on your part and all of your hard work is wasted. You could have the greatest process, product, customer service, web site, you name it—everything could be great. But you make him not OK, you could just as well be selling trash. He won't buy.

> When you are sincerely OK with any outcome, you are well on your way to keeping your prospect psychologically OK.
>
> *BILL CASKEY*

If you're engaged in traditional sales techniques, I promise you this: you are not keeping your prospect OK. You are leaning on him. You are exerting pressure. Sure, it may not be much pressure—but it is enough that he's not sharing the truth with you about several things: why you're there in the first place, what he's going to do to fix the problem, how severe the problem is, and what he'll spend to get rid of it.

RULE

Your income will rise in direct proportion to how psychologically OK you keep your prospect during the buying process.

Find yourself saying often:

- *Gee, it looks like you have everything under control here.*
- *I'm not really sure I can help you.*
- *I'm not sure I hear anything which would compel you to change from your current system.*
- *Is it OK if I ask you some questions?*
- *Are you going to be OK with that?*
- *Is that appropriate for you?*
- *It's really OK if you want to end this right now.*

- *My goal is to help you solve a problem—but if you have other sources of solutions, then maybe you should go with them. I really need to know more before I can tell you if I can help.*

And watch him come around.

Keep your prospect OK by not pushing him at anytime during the process. Always make sure they know you are OK if they decide you are not the solution.

All of these things will keep your prospect feeling safe and wanting to share more of what will compel him to make the change, purchase or commitment. The more he shares with you, the better the connection between his problem and your solution.

I have a client who likens the way most traditional salespeople sell to "bringing out the pots and pans." He says when the prospect starts to show even the slightest interest, most amateur salespeople start to lay out their pots and pans on the table. Don't bring out your pots and pans too soon.

Here's How it Works

Your income goes up when you make a sale. You won't make a sale if the prospect doesn't see your value. He won't see your value if he can't attach what you do to some pain or condition affecting him now. And he won't see that if he can't come to grips with what that condition is and get out of denial about the condition. And that won't occur unless you can keep him OK while you're getting that pain from him.

Stuart Wilde makes an excellent point in his book, *The Trick to Money is Having Some*. Here are his words:

> *In order to successfully serve people you have to get underneath them psychologically, which means that while you are serving them you have to subjugate*

your ego to their needs long enough to take their money.

Once you set aside your ego needs long enough, your prospect will be more open with you about his problems and be more attracted to your solution. See how easy this is? Keep him OK and go to the bank.

A C T I O N   I T E M

Based on that, here is a thought for the initiate: during the first call or meeting with a prospect (especially if you are in the longer cycle sale—thirty days or more) make one goal for yourself. Keep him psychologically OK. Yes, even if he is the type to want to take control and make you not OK (which many people do if they see you as a salesperson with ulterior motives) keep your focus on "keeping him OK." How do you do it? What is the one thing you will say on your next call—today— that will help keep your prospect OK? This insight had many examples. Pick one.

THE MORE YOU TALK, THE MORE LIKELY YOU ARE TO SAY SOMETHING STUPID

OLD THINKING	NEW THINKING
If I talk a lot, I'm in control and people see how smart I am.	If I listen more, I'm in control. I'm also less likely to bring up something to which my prospect can object.

I had a mentor who told me, "It's impossible for your prospect to object to you if you give him nothing to object to." He had a point. The less you say, the less hope the prospect has of finding that one thing that they can object to.

But the fact is, you have to say something. To make a buying decision, your prospect must have some data and facts—some gut sense that you understand his problem and can fix it prior to him moving forward. So what is the correct amount of talking you should do in the process?

You should be talking 25% of the time and your prospect should be talking 75% of the time. That's right. He should be talking three times more than you should. Not all at once, of course, but over the span of a one-hour sales call those percentages should hold firm. Why is this? Three reasons:

1. If you're talking, you aren't hearing his problems and opportunities. Isn't that why you're there in the first place? To hear his issues? And by telling you those issues, doesn't he become even more aware of their seriousness? A good psychotherapist will tell you that unless the client is revealing and verbalizing the problem, it's not a problem. Or at least it's not a problem that the client is ready and willing to change. So, you're the therapist. Your goal is to have him associate his problem to your solution.

> A fool talks while
> a wise man thinks.
>
> *Oxford Dictionary
> for American Proverbs*

2. When he's talking he'll begin to reveal incremental information to you, which will help you in the sales process. Our mouths move faster than our brains. Consequently, when you ask your prospect good questions, you'll begin getting information from him at a much deeper level. Just relax and listen. That information will help steer the process for you.

3. People love to talk about themselves. I'm frequently asked, "Won't my prospects get upset if I ask them all kinds of detailed questions about their problems?" My answer is always, "Prospects would rather talk about their problems than listen to your features and benefits any day." So in essence, you're keeping them OK even though you may be asking them questions about

problems in their lives around your product. People love to talk, so let 'em.

I'm also asked about closed-ended and open-ended questions—which is right or wrong? Don't get hung up on that. If your intent is to help the prospect solve a problem and you do that by keeping him OK, what difference does it make?

As you continue to work on creating the optimum environment in which your prospect reveals his pains to you, you'll begin to accumulate emotional data that your competition won't acquire. If they knew this method they could. However, they probably won't take the time to study it like you will.

> The less you talk,
> the more you're listened to.
>
> ABIGAIL VAN BUREN

While you are busy listening to prospects, your competitor is spouting off features and benefits and talking about how great they are. Maybe they are the best, but you'll get the sale.

One of my clients told me, "The more emotion I can evoke from my prospect, the higher the odds that he'll connect his current problem to my solution."

A C T I O N   I T E M

Go out and buy a tape recorder and record some telephone calls to your prospects and clients. Then play the tape back and it will reveal how much you really do talk. You may think you're listening seventy-five percent of the time, but take out the stopwatch and you may find a different story. Quite often we're in denial about how much we listen. An objective tape recorder can help us see what's really occurring. If the law prohibits you from taping both parties, just tape your side of the conversation. It will also tell how quick you are to bring out your "pots and pans."

THERE IS WISDOM IN IGNORANCE

OLD THINKING	NEW THINKING
The more I know and the smarter I look, the more likely my prospect will be to buy.	I keep what I know to myself. I only share my knowledge when it's in our mutual interest to do so.

There are occasions when the highest wisdom consists in appearing not to know—you must not be ignorant but capable of playing it.

—BALTASAR GRACIAN

Isn't it interesting how many hours we spend reading and studying how to be smart, how to look smart, how to dress smart and how to act superior to those we meet? Did you ever think that the very thing we were trying to accomplish in our formative years in school—intellectual superiority—was really our undoing in sales?

In sales, you're looking to control the process, which exists to help prospects reveal to you their inner-most pains, frustrations and needs. You want them to be open, honest and sincere with you in a world that defies safety.

R U L E

Appearing too smart is in nobody's best interest.

You're not looking to be a threat, but to be a beacon of safety in the brutal world of business. So, why do you go about it all wrong? Trust me, you're not alone when you devise silly ways to look good, credible, and secure and feel intellectually superior at a time when your real strength is in being a little less secure—a little less intellectually superior. You must have power over the process, and sometimes that power is in not being too smart—not having all of the answers.

> He who overcomes others is strong. But he who overcomes himself is mightier.
>
> *JOHN HENRY PATTERSON*

In sales, this means you need to start with a clean slate. Let him paint the picture of his problem. Ask why the prospect feels the way he does. Ask basic questions. Ask what he thinks you should do next. Ask questions from a place of curiosity—not from a place of manipulation. Even if you know the answer to your prospect's question, preserve his integrity by not answering for him. Keep the power—and through that, you will create a better environment for your prospect to open up and tell you how to sell him.

Your previous experience in your business should be used only as a basis for the right questions to ask—not for the right answers to those questions. Maybe you've spoken with 99 other prospects that have similar business pains.

Don't be an amateur and assume you understand the motivation of the 100th person. When you assume, you block him from telling you the truth, and end up with misinformation. When you practice this insight, you can be sure you're getting the truth from your prospect.

Count up how many clients you have, and I'll guess each one of them buys for a very different reason. Their needs may be the same, but the impact of that need—the pain—will be different. Don't you agree that a great injustice is done to you both when you fail to ask the right questions?

> Never assume the obvious is true.
>
> **WILLIAM SAFIRE**
> *Sleeper Spy*

In the previous insight, we told you that the psychotherapist wants the client to verbalize problems because he learned early he is in the belief-change business. And we know that no one changes belief until they first admit they have a problem.

Knowing that there's wisdom in ignorance is the best way to get the flow of information moving in the right direction—from your prospect to you.

Tactic

Here is a tactic which honors this insight. When you're meeting with a potential client and just beginning to ask questions, try saying this:

> *Chris, as you may know, I've been in this industry for twelve years and my experience tells me there are always things I know and things I don't know. What I know is that we've helped many companies like yours that are hoping to either reduce costs or increase margins by looking at different management tools. But what I don't know is if either of these benefits*

*would be of any value to you—and if so, how open
you would be to discussing them.*

With this approach, you're letting your prospect educate you. That's the way it should be. He tells you his problems, and you tell him if you can fix them. Isn't that more elegant than you telling him all of your great features and him giving you objections?

ACTION ITEMS

In the next week, use the above tactic five times in the appropriate situation. Role-play it with a colleague or with yourself prior to trying it in the marketplace. Or, use the tape recorder you used earlier in the book to hear how you sound when you deliver it. Email me and let me know how it worked: **info@samegamenewrules.com**

PROSPECTS ARE PEOPLE FIRST

OLD THINKING	NEW THINKING
I'm talking to the purchasing agent.	I'm talking to a person who happens to be the purchasing agent.

We forget that we are selling to a person—not a sales manager, or a CEO, or a department head with budgetary responsibility. We are selling to a person who wakes up in the morning, worries about the day, wants to care for a family and who goes to bed at night thinking, "Is my job safe? Is this what I want to be doing forever? Am I achieving my potential?"

You must understand the human perspective. Buying is emotional. You must take care of your prospect's emotional needs. Most of us work in a stroke-free environment—compliments are scarce. So when you show up, remember that. Acknowledge people's achievements and previous decisions, even if the decisions didn't involve you.

In the total scheme of things, you are calling on yourself. Think about the things you're afraid of, that you're anxious about, that you want to avoid talking about—and those very things are what they wrestle with as well.

> I now perceive one immense omission in my Psychology—the deepest craving of human nature is the craving to be appreciated.
>
> **WILLIAM JAMES**
> *Letters*

When you ask a salesperson whom he calls on, he'll undoubtedly say the VP of Purchasing, or the Director of IT. While that may be correct intellectually, you need to consider that a prospect is still a human being first and a VP second.

Remember that you are always calling on yourself. Whatever worries you have, he has. Whatever pains you have, he has. Whatever dreams you have, he has. When you can see yourself across the desk from you, your technique will change—as will the results.

NEVER ASK QUESTIONS THAT FORCE YOUR PROSPECT TO LIE

OLD THINKING	NEW THINKING
I'll just ask a bunch of open-ended questions.	Questions are worthless unless they are the right questions, asked the right way to the right people.

All sales trainers teach you to ask more questions. I, however, want you to ask fewer questions—especially if they're to the wrong people. In my work with salespeople, I see them ask great questions—but of the wrong people. What do you suppose happens when you ask the right question to the wrong person?

At least two things—neither of them with good results:

1. People are forced to cover their tracks. If you ask a purchasing manager what the vision of the company

is, and they don't know (which they probably won't), they'll construct something so as not to sound stupid. And it will probably be something which is self-serving like, "Our vision is to buy as cheap as we can and cut out the middle-men suppliers." (Also known as you.)

What are you going to say to that? You can't fight him on it—after all, that is his opinion. You must then deal with it. Once it's out there in the physical world as an observation, it will slow the sales process.

2. People will become not OK. Meaning, when someone asks you a question to which you don't know the answer, you probably won't admit you don't know. Instead, you'll instinctively take your hostility out on the person who put you in the situation in the first place. It happens quickly and is very difficult to undo once done.

Before you ask your prospect questions, make sure the person has a good chance of answering them. If you're talking to the president of the company, ask about the company's vision and their biggest obstacle in accomplishing that. But if you're speaking with the VP of Operations, the question should be different: "What is your biggest challenge as you grow or improve your department?" Or, "Related to the vision of the company, what is your biggest challenge?"

> The greatest obstacle to discovering the shape of the earth, the continents and the ocean is not ignorance, but the illusion of knowledge.
>
> DANIEL BOORSTIN

That way, you get the question asked, and still have half a chance of getting a good answer. The rule in law is to never ask a question in court to which you don't know the answer. While there is no way you can ever know the answer to everything, the point in law is to be very, very careful which questions you ask. In sales, you may get an answer that hurts you later, because it may not be the truth.

R U L E

Never ask a question that forces a lie.

Salespeople think all they need to do is ask a bunch of leading questions. They have been taught that when the prospect is talking, the sale is progressing and that when the prospect is listening, they are in control. Some of that is true. But *how* you ask these questions is more important than what you ask.

The wrong way to ask is to interrogate. It will appear that you're trying to get the prospect

> "How do you like what you have?" This is a question anybody can ask anybody. Ask it.
>
> GERTRUDE STEIN

to say something that you can slap him with later. There are two types of questions—intellectual and emotional. Intellectual questions are based in fact.

How many units do you currently buy?
How many times have you had the problem?
Who else makes this decision?
When did you buy last?
What colors did you buy?

Virtually any kind of "how" questions will lead you to intellectual answers. Emotional questions, on the other hand, are more important. These should center on "why."

Why did you decide to invite me in?
Why are you looking at doing this now?
Why is this so important to you?
Why do you care about this at your company?

Here's an example of the type of information you'll get when you ask these four emotional questions. Listen to the responses and see if this is what you want.

WHY DID YOU DECIDE TO INVITE ME IN?

Prospect: Your call came at a time when we were examining our options. We have been wrestling with this the last three years, and we really need to do something.

WHY ARE YOU LOOKING AT DOING THIS NOW?

Prospect: We've been dealing with this problem for three years. That's a long time to deal with any problem and if we don't get this fixed within the next year, we're going to be dealing with intense competitive pressures.

WHY IS THIS SO IMPORTANT TO YOU?

Prospect: I'm the head of the department, and I get reviewed every year on improvements and innovations. This would be a huge feather in my cap if I could pull this off in the next twelve months. Plus, I've got other things that demand my attention. This is wearing me out.

WHY DO YOU CARE ABOUT THIS AT YOUR COMPANY?

Prospect: We're trying to be a market leader. Our vision is to have a sixty-percent market share in the next five years. If we can't get this problem solved, we can kiss that vision good-bye!

Do you see the difference? Do you see how "why" questions give you answers to which you can ask further questions? And that "how" questions only give you dead-end answers?

How many units do you currently buy?—"100."
How many times have you had the problem?—"Three
times."

Through this whole process you are actually helping your customer put into perspective why you were invited in, and what value you can bring to their organization. Your biggest value comes by asking the right questions and helping them connect your solution to their problem.

The questions you ask will provide true insight into their thinking processes and reasons for meeting with you. Chances are your competition won't be asking these questions. They'll be back in the "how," while you're successfully navigating through the "why."

"But I've been taught 'why' questions are intrusive."

Don't believe it. It simply isn't true. If you ask these questions in the right way—with a fair amount of nurturing and good tonality—and you really do care about the answer to your "why" questions, then they will answer them. I'm flattered when someone asks me a "why" question. It gives me a chance to tell them about me at a deeper level.

Lastly, you must nurture people as you ask. You must tell them when you're going to ask a tough question. For example, when you want to discover the answer to, "Why are you looking at doing this?" Maybe your style won't permit you to ask it like that, so try this:

Mr. Smith, I always like to ask the question of why
you're looking at this now. It helps give me insight into
your motivations. So, can I ask you that? What was it
that prompted you to be interested in this in the first
place?

A C T I O N   I T E M

Let's suppose you're talking with a potential client (first meeting). Come up with five "why" questions that lead you to important information you need to know in order to continue. Here are two to get you started:

1. Why did you happen to invite me in to your office today?
2. I'm not sure I understand why that is a problem for you.

3. _____

4. _____

5. _____

Effortless Conversation Breaks Down Resistance

OLD THINKING	NEW THINKING
When the prospect starts giving me buying signals, I react by getting excited.	When they sound like they're interested, I withhold my zeal. When they sound like they aren't interested, I withhold my pressure.

The new breed of seller is looking to collaborate, not to persuade. The ability to have an effortless dialogue with your prospect—not selling or convincing—but conversing, will break down any resistance that could arise. Remember—you aren't looking to sell anyone anything until you see a possibility for a "fit."

In sales there will always be times when you'll say something to a prospect or potential client that they'll resist. They will disbelieve your point or what you're saying. Regardless of how hard you argue, or intellectualize, they will refuse to see things your way. In fact, quite often, just because you seem so attached to your opinion, they will refuse it. It sometimes must seem to them that you are so entrenched in your position that you are closed-minded and unable to see theirs.

> Patience! The windmill never strays in search of the wind.
>
> **ANDY SKLIVIS**

In that case, the very thing you are looking for them to be—open-minded—won't come naturally because you're as closed-minded as they are. In those cases, you must use the Law of Ebb and Flow. The Law of Ebb and Flow is a human dynamic which tells you what goes up must come down—what goes out must come back and what goes negative must return positive.

In a discussion between two people, you and your prospect, the law is always at work. By forcing the conversation to a place you want it to go, you may be preventing it from getting there.

> The key to everything is patience. You get the chicken by hatching the egg, not by smashing it.
>
> **ARNOLD GLASOW**

When you honor the law you'll find yourself in the same place as your prospect. If they are full of disbelief, you must find yourself saying things like, "I don't blame you. Perhaps this isn't right for you," or "I just thought this might be something you wanted to look at, but the fact is I have plenty of things in the works and the last thing I was trying to do was sell you. Should we just quit?" If they're full of doubt, you're full of doubt. If they're skeptical, you're skeptical.

Don't let yourself revert to previous training, which says, "Enthusiasm is contagious."

"Convince harder."

"Sell harder."

"Be more positive."

So, if you have a prospect who is skeptical or negative, the Law of Ebb and Flow says that he can't stay in that mind-set for very long. He must start moving back to center or to a less negative position. Never give the prospect anything to dig his heels in against. You will only move him further away from you.

> A certain amount of opposition is a great help to a man. Kites rise against, not with, the wind.
>
> JOHN NEAL

People want to be right. You want to because your ego is screaming at you sixteen hours a day to "be right." Your prospect wants to be right as well—so let him.

R U L E

Don't let your ego's need to be right leave you in poverty.

Drop back. Let the conversation and his position ebb and flow, until it moves back in your direction. It will, especially if you've treated him right through the first parts of the process and are truly interested in helping him find and solve a problem. If you're not, you shouldn't be there.

Now that you know the law, make it work for you. The power you have—now that you have enlightenment around this element—will work for you until it becomes intuitive.

Do not care if you sell anything—only be in tune and connected with your prospect's problems. Then you'll make the sale on your terms—with no discounting. Isn't that what you want?

Here's an example:

Prospect:	You know, I'm not really sure we want to buy this at this time. We have a lot of other things going on and we just don't have the time to devote to it.
You:	I totally understand. Maybe this isn't the right time. The last thing I want to do is create more problems for you. You told me last month that you had some severe problems you were trying to solve, but now it sounds like those have disappeared. (You know they haven't, but you must always go back to the original "compelling reason.")
Prospect:	No, they really haven't gone away. I just don't know if this is the time to solve them.
You:	I don't either. Sounds like that leaves us a couple of choices. One, we can stop and forget we even started this. I can go on to my next project and you can continue dealing with the problem. Or, we can start over and figure out if this problem is really something you want to fix. I must tell you that I'm OK with either outcome.
Prospect:	No, the problem still hasn't been fixed. And it still is a serious problem. I suppose we should continue.

Remember, if there were problems discussed earlier in the process, you must always go back to those. Keep them on the table in front of him. If you don't, all he'll see is more trouble in fixing them than the original problem cost.

Do you see how you can keep your prospect psychologically OK using the Law of Ebb and Flow to keep the conversation moving? By not getting nervous or excited, or exerting pressure to "convince" prospects to change their beliefs, you can lead your prospect exactly where you want to go.

The Law of Ebb and Flow will make your selling life easier.

A C T I O N   I T E M

Make a list of the types of objections you get early in the process—too busy to talk to you, happy with current supplier, etc. Come up with a sample of the ebb and flow that would take place if you just stepped back and relaxed, without trying to change his mind.

Curiosity is one
of the permanent and
certain characteristics
of a vigorous intellect.

SAMUEL JOHNSON

YOUR NEED FOR APPROVAL WILL COST YOU THOUSANDS

OLD THINKING	NEW THINKING
If I can get them to like me, they might buy from me.	I'm in the selling profession to help my prospects solve problems. The only approval that matters to me is that which I get from myself—when I know I've carried out that mission.

Most salespeople feel that they need to be liked before they can sell anything to a prospect or a client. They erroneously believe that the odds of making the sale go up when they can coerce approval from the prospect. On the surface this seems quite rational and logical, but let's look into the abyss of human nature to discover the truth.

The root of the need for approval comes from your childhood. When you were young, you got strokes and rewards for doing well in your life's roles. Those roles included activities like sports, school, sibling behavior and the hundreds of other roles you took on. Consequently, you realized quickly that part of your compensation in life was tied to the approval you got from external sources—parents, teachers, friends and other authority figures.

For example, when you brought home an "A" from school, you got strokes. They were conditional, but still felt good. You loved hearing your dad say, "Great job! I knew you were smart enough to get A's. You really are a good kid."

> The simulated approval and affection with which parents and teachers are often urged to solve behavior problems are counterfeit. So are flattery, back-slapping and "many other ways of winning friends."
>
> **B.F. SKINNER**
> *Beyond Freedom and Dignity*

As we grew older we never forgot how good that felt, and we continued to modify our behavior and actions to create more of those good feelings through approval. Dorothy Briggs wrote a wonderful book called *Celebrate Your Self*, in which she chronicles the approval seeking experience:

> *The source for the approval we need as adults is our "child's" need for parental approval. In adulthood we turn all others into substitute parents . . .*

I'll bet you never thought of your client or prospect as a parental figure. But if we enter the process in a state of need, asking for something from them, how is that really much different than the scenarios we experienced at an early age of begging our parents for candy—or to play outside—or to watch another hour of TV?

The role of the seller in traditional circles is a "child-like" role. You are the child. Your potential client is the parent. We must change that traditional role. The way to change it is to have awareness that the prospect is not our parent—we do not need his approval. We want to help him solve a problem, but only if he is in pain.

No Payday in Approval

In the business world, getting people to like you doesn't translate into payday. But because of our prior conditioning, we still tie the two together. Now, don't jump to conclusions and think we're suggesting that you should anger people intentionally. Whether people like you or not shouldn't matter. What should matter is whether they see you as a solution to their pain and problems.

> We seek our happiness outside ourselves and in the opinion of men whom we know to be flatterers, insincere, unjust, full of envy, caprice and prejudice. How absurd!
>
> *JEAN DE LA BRUYERE*

In fact, if you do provide them the solution to their pain or problem they will like you more—even more than the guy that is outwardly seeking their approval in the beginning.

In other words, it's the order that is important.

The Old Way

I get him to like me first, then I can sell him.

The New Way

I get him to open up and tell me his problems, and by me fixing them he will ask me to solve more. Approval doesn't enter into it.

Approval Script

In psychology, a script is a set of actions in which you engage following a certain stimuli. The script is like a cue that triggers a certain response in your mind. Whether it is fear, excitement or anxiety, we all have situations that elicit certain internal responses in our brains. In fact, most of these responses are subconscious—we don't even know our script is running. But these aren't just feelings or emotions—they are a distinct set of actions we run through to cope with the stimuli.

To help you see it clearer, let me explain exactly how the need for approval manifests itself in the selling process. In my experience it comes out in different stages throughout the beginning, middle and end.

THE BEGINNING

The highest likelihood for rejection comes in the first one to five minutes when making your first call on a person. That's the first place you can be rejected. So, as you prepare for the call, your childhood scripts will kick in "Watch out! Huge danger! Likely rejection!" And, to totally avoid the rejection, you may not even make the call—or, make fewer

> Please all and you will please none.
>
> *AESOP*

than needed. When you don't make the call, your prospect doesn't get his pain fixed or problem solved, and you don't get his money. Everyone is a loser.

THE MIDDLE

Even if you get past the need for approval in the beginning and get a face-to-face meeting with your prospect, you aren't out of the woods yet. The approval problem comes up during the information exchange—the dialogue between you and the prospect. Where the need for approval hinders you is in the process of asking very tough, difficult and sensitive questions of the prospect.

For many of us it is easy to get past the up-front approval problem because that person is still a stranger to us. You might say to yourself, "I don't really care if strangers don't like me." And for some that is true.

But as you continue through the sales process, you begin to develop a relationship with this prospect. After a couple of meetings, you start to move into a friendship role with this person. At that very time, it becomes even more dangerous for you to ask those tough questions, because approval may be withheld by a "friend." In the middle of the sales process, the need for approval and this inability to ask tough questions comes out in three ways.

> Don't compromise yourself. You are all you've got.
>
> *JANIS JOPLIN*

1. It's Difficult to Get the Uncomfortable Questions Out of Our Mouths.

We all have areas we tend to avoid. Some salespeople avoid talking about money. Some hate asking about the decision-making process. Some don't want to know too much—they're afraid they won't know how to handle what the prospect gives them. When you don't ask the question, you withhold from your prospect the catalyst for connecting his problem with your solution.

2. It's Hard to Challenge Someone's Response.

Too often we take whatever the prospect says as law, even though our gut screams at us, "Hey, what he said doesn't make sense." We fear that if we bring up the topic for further discussion, he will get mad at us and, ultimately, get rid of us—another blow to our approval need. Consequently, we wind up losing the deal because we don't get the proper information. It didn't happen because the prospect lied to us or because we didn't know what to ask. It happened because we were frightened of what the prospect might think if we were to challenge him.

3. WE'RE TOO AFRAID TO ADDRESS PROBLEMS UP-FRONT.

You've been there. You've made a couple of calls on your prospect and suddenly he says, "Fine, give me a quote and if it's in line, I'll switch from ABC to you." While your inner child is jumping up and down saying, "We got it!," your more intuitive voice is full of caution. And you know from experience that when your prospect goes to

> In life, our self has become divided in two. One is our **true** self, what we were born with. What is inside our skin. What we will take with us. The second is our **role** self, a combination of societal roles and material acquisitions. The most effective place from which to operate is the **true** self.
>
> *PARKER PALMER*

their long-time current vendor and tells them they're switching, the vendor's price drops immediately.

So why don't you bring it up? You know you should. It's the right thing at the right time. What stops you is the need for approval. Your inner voice says, "I know I should ask, but what if he gets mad at me and doesn't buy from me? At least I still have a chance now!"

The End

Finally, it's common for approval to get in the way near the end of the selling process. We'll call this the "hanging-on phase." It's in the "think it over" or "maybe" phase, when the prospect tells us, "I need to think about it," or "I'll get back to you." We don't challenge them at all.

Instead we come back with, "Well OK, I'll look forward to hearing from you." We're afraid to say, "Well, I need to hear back from you by next Tuesday, or I've got to pull my proposal." We're afraid we'll lose the deal and they won't like us. The real problem happened when we failed to lay out the process for the prospect and we lost control. It's hard to detach from approval at the end because of the amount of time we've already invested.

How to Change

So now that we know what the problems are, how do we go about changing them? The first step in fixing an approval script is to become aware of the precise point of occurrence in your selling process. Start to identify where you feel the most anxiety, or where you feel the need to be liked is the strongest. For some it's the beginning, for some it's the middle, and for others, the end.

A good test will be to read back through the examples we gave, and become aware of when it happens to you.

Second, begin listening to your gut and to your subconscious communication. Hear the inner voice of caution as you prepare to engage in risky behavior. Begin listening to that intuition and your gut more than you have in the past.

> Chase after money and security and your heart will never unclench. Care about people's approval and you will be their prisoner.
>
> *TAO TE CHING*

Third, engage in that risky behavior. If you are going to change results dramatically you have to begin to engage in a behavior that feels risky or frightening in the beginning.

The fourth step is to own your feeling to the prospect. If your prospect has just said something that you feel needs to be challenged, but your need for approval prohibits you from bringing it up, you must gather the courage to tell the prospect, "I'm a little bit uncomfortable bringing this up, Steve, but feel it's the right thing to do at this time. You said. . . ."

Take an honest assessment of the situations where you're anxious about approval from others and notice how you react to those. Is it when you're asked to make a big presentation? Is it on a first call? Is it at a networking function? It's a shame to have the best solution and best product in the world, but not be able to make the sale because you were afraid to ask the question that would help your prospect connect his problem with your solution.

Understand the Laws of Money

OLD THINKING	NEW THINKING
If I sell harder, I can convince people my product is worth buying.	I realize that there are principles of money, which govern how it gets transferred between people. I want to understand those laws so I can leverage them, rather than fight them.

I am about to suggest something that flies in the face of every sales quota you've ever tried to meet:

Stop Trying to Get Your Customer's Money

By obeying and honoring certain undeniable laws of money, you can help your clients feel more comfortable while at the same time helping your income and your company grow significantly.

Law #1

The less you care about money, the more you'll make.

There are five million sales managers in this country who have a Bob working for them. The purpose of this is to lay out what typically happens when thinking is wrong.

Bob's sales manager had just finished his annual review. And while his numbers were off a little this year, Bob was still a good performer. But his manager had said something during the review that bothered him. "Bob, we've given you some pretty good leads lately and you haven't closed any of them. Is there a problem?"

He replied, "No, I'm just in a little slump, I guess. It will change next week though. I have a lead for the Backer Corporation—I really think they're a good prospect."

Naturally, this conversation created tension for Bob. His manager had never asked him that question before. So, by the time he arrived at the Backer appointment he had worked himself into a state of desperation. Consequently, the Bob who made the call that day was a needy Bob ready to plead with and/or coerce his soon-to-be defensive and unwilling client. The result—no sale.

When you become needy of money or business, you push away the very people who can help you. When you must have the sale, you'll fall into a hard sell of product features, quickly raising your client's wall of resistance and leaving you with either a meager sale or none at all. Similarly, your

> People have to be secure to transfer their money to you. Never forget that. How you make them secure is to not come at them from above telling them how marvelous the product is and how marvelous you are. Instead, work on their comfort zone first . . . leading things along effortlessly by asking questions.
>
> *STUART WILDE*
> *The Infinite Self*

needy image will turn off your best prospects and leave you with those who are as needy as you are.

If you approach your client with more interest in solving problems than getting money, and the client is someone you can and want to help, you'll get more business and money than you ever thought possible. Why? Because you're approaching your client as a human being and focusing on his challenges rather than your own. By doing so, you create trust and a real relationship that will ultimately pay more dividends than the most ardent begging or convincing hard sell.

> To every one who has will be more given and he will have abundance, but from him who has not, even what he has will be taken away.
>
> MATTHEW 25:29 KJV

Law #2

Push your clients too hard and their money will leave with them.

Many sales trainers will teach you to push your clients to the point of decision from the beginning of the process. The trouble with this is, people hate to be pushed. Eventually, your client simply shuts down in defense, which is the very opposite of what you want him to do—open up. There are times when you need to get a decision—for example when the process has gone on too long, and you need to sell or move on. Then you can force decisions. But not up front.

Your goal should be to create an environment in which your client pulls you along. The optimum strategy is to have your prospect selling you on why he needs you. At your first call, simply lay out your intent with a non-threatening, servant-like attitude: "My intent today is to understand why you called me in and what your problems are, and we'll see if I can help you. If not, I'll try to point you to where you might find the right help."

By saying this, you give your prospect permission to open up and lead you through his challenges, so you can discover if you can address those problems. If not, have the dignity to say so. If so, share your solutions when appropriate (Insight 23).

> Education is not
> the filling of the bucket,
> but the starting of a fire.
>
> **WILLIAM BUTLER YEATS**

Resist the temptation to close the deal. Often, the amateur will go through this initial process only to blurt out something like "Sounds great, John! I've got just what you need. Can we work together?" Even when you know you can help, continue to explore options with your client, allowing him to pull you along. Never get more excited than your prospect.

Law #3

If you trap your clients, they'll run.

When you pursue a sale in the traditional way, you in essence stand over your clients, trapping them so that there is nowhere for them to go but out the door. Your goal should always be to leave your client an escape hatch.

If you move underneath your client psychologically, you allow them room to express their pain and problems as they move upward and take you with them. It's the difference between the old technique—"I have what's best for you" and the new technique—"I'm not sure if I'm a fit for you, but let's find out." One attitude traps customers in a patronizing way; the other serves your customers and lets them discover how you can best help them.

Law #4

Never be afraid to talk about money.

Just as you shouldn't focus on money when working with a client, neither should you completely ignore it. If you hide the costs of your products or services until the end of the sales process, you create an easy objection for your prospect.

Understand your prospect's pain and situation. If you sense that money will be a problem, bring it up early, not to make a sale but to ensure that neither you nor your prospect waste time or embarrass each other. With every potential client, lay out your process and discover your prospect's challenges in your first meeting, saying that you'll discuss costs at your second visit (or whenever it should occur in your process) and that, if cost creates a problem, you'll both know you shouldn't go any further.

> Money is a good servant, but a bad master.
>
> *FRENCH PROVERB*

If you approach the topic of money from a place of respect, it will just be a part of building your relationship. You can only achieve this, however, if you truly believe it's OK that not everyone will buy from you. Tell your prospect that it's all right if he can't proceed with you, and mean it. If your process moves forward from there, it will be from a point of increased trust and honor. If not, you'll have saved time and saved yourself and your client from a relationship that is not a proper fit. You are in control of the process— never forget that.

Law #5

If you want to raise income and revenues significantly, you must think differently.

Too frequently, companies and individuals decide they're going to earn more money without figuring out how they'll change in order to do it. Few of us can earn twice as much money by working twice as hard. Even if you could, would you be willing to give up that much of your personal and family time? You probably work forty to sixty hours a week right now if you're like me. I can't imagine investing 120 hours a week to double my income. So to earn more, I must think differently.

The key to earning more money, then, is to earn it differently. It may mean giving up key customers or well-established business practices. It could mean reframing the way you generate leads. But most importantly, it will involve a new thought process. Money follows thought, and if you want to grow twenty five percent, you'll have to do more than change your tactics. You'll have to change the entire way you think about your career and your business.

Money is an emotional subject. Our society doesn't teach kids how to earn money, and parents rarely inform their children of their income. Think back for a second. When did your parents sit you down and have a long discussion about the family income and financial goals? How old were you when you had that family meeting? What? You never had it? I didn't either. It just isn't something people are comfortable talking about. Because we were never taught it was OK to talk about money, most of us handle the subject ineptly, often with force, apology or avoidance.

Take the emotion out of money. Detach yourself from your desire for it. Know that if one prospect doesn't buy from you, another will. Approach it with both quiet confidence in your product and with compassionate concern for your prospects and their problems. If you can ease your prospect's pain, you'll make the sale and create an honest partnership that will reap rewards for both of you.

A C T I O N   I T E M

Look right now at the prospects you have in your funnel and mark those that you feel could be unclear about money—either the money you charge or the financial impact of your solution. Make a phone call and say the following: "Mr. Walters, as I was looking over our notes from last week (or whenever), I realized that we never really quantified either the problem you have, or the solution I have. And I'm very uncomfortable about that. Could we set up a time when we can talk about both of those issues so that we both have a good understanding of why we're doing this?"

By doing that, you can begin to reprogram your thinking about money and the taboo-ness of the subject.

MONEY ARRIVES WHEN YOU'RE READY

OLD THINKING	NEW THINKING
Selling is selling. It has to do with products and features. That's it.	I realize that if I am to experience a quantum leap in my income, I must be mentally ready for it. I had better prepare my self-image so that I can accept it with grace.

When I entered the training business in 1990, I focused heavily on the tactics and strategies of selling. After all, that's what people were crying for—better ways to prospect, better methods of advancing deals, more effective ways to manage the sales process. Companies wanted it. Salespeople wanted it.

As I worked with thousands of people in virtually every industry, I got a deep sense of something even more ethereal occurring that was equally responsible for the profound success I was helping some people achieve. It wasn't only about techniques and approaches and strategies, it was about the inner game of money, income, and success, however one defines it. At our first meeting under contract, I would pull out a prop—my magic wand. As I handed it to my new client, here's what I said:

> *This is a magic wand. It is magic because when you have it in your hand, you have the power to create any future you desire. Based on that, what is it that you want to create?*

I thought this was a relatively simple exercise. My point in doing it was to get them to think to the future—outside the daily box of appointments, quotas, and challenging prospects. It was a question my mentor asked me whenever we'd talk. But instead of peace, quiet and passion, I got something entirely different from most people. It generated shock, surprise and in most cases some real pain. When I saw this reaction, I asked deeper questions. When was the last time someone asked you what you wanted your future to look like? Who asked it of you? Has your answer changed since then? How do you feel about the question?

> The Universe's true nature, that of infinite abundance, reveals itself when you let go of your own perceptions.
>
> **BILL CASKEY**

The answers gave me a deeper insight into human behavior and motivation. Often, I found the success my clients were having before I worked with them was marginal only because they weren't giving themselves permission to raise their income. They had never thought about their future as a picture. The magic wand exercise caused a **conscious connection** between the reality they wanted to create and a belief that that reality was possible. All that was left then was the challenge of breaking through the layers of limitations and baggage. (In Insight 5, you were asked to create your vision of your income, your account type, and your optimum process.)

What Began to Happen

Success started to come easier. They created revenue for their companies and income for themselves because they were prepared for it. In fact, the strugglers—those that hadn't wanted to do the exercise—always seemed to be working harder. They seemed to be rushing about creating a whirlwind of activity, yet never quite busting out of their comfort zone. To them, busy-ness was an end.

As my high-achieving clients began to get comfortable with their future picture, their minds shifted. Their confidence soared. More doors were opened—and with less effort. They saw opportunities they didn't see before. They started calling on people they wouldn't have spoken to last week. They demanded to see the CEO because that was their new nature. As they became more OK with wealth, their tactics and strategies began to mirror their newfound confidence and wealth came easier.

> Never endorse a thought form of scarcity or lack in your circumstances and further, never endorse the poverty of others.
>
> STUART WILDE
> *The Trick to Money is Having Some*

A Story Honoring the Insight

One of my clients is a financial planner. He runs a firm that specializes in helping people create and grow wealth. He let me in on a secret of financial planning which fits nicely with this insight. He said that when people create a financial plan early in life, research shows they will create significantly more wealth than the individual without a plan. When I asked him why, he had an astonishing answer. He told me it wasn't because they merely had the plan or forced themselves to contribute to it. It was more than discipline.

> All truly wise thoughts have been thought already thousands of times. But to make them truly ours, we must think them over again honestly 'til they take root in our personal experience.
>
> JOHANN WOLFGANG
> von GOETHE

People with wealth plans have given themselves *psychological permission* to make their plan a reality. They have made themselves OK with achieving and accomplishing their goal. And because they are more OK, the attraction of that wealth becomes easier, quicker and without hassle. The plan and the thinking process they go through when they build it acts as a pipeline to the wealth they want to acquire. Once the plan is built, the cash has an easier time showing up.

On the other hand, people without a plan still earn money—sometimes good money—but that money has a tendency to disappear. It is as if they don't feel they deserve it so they waste it away a little at a time. Their money's gone—out the window, spent on things that don't matter. And they wake up in a panic at 55 because they see they'll fall short financially at retirement.

A definitive plan for wealth makes it OK if wealth shows up. It's almost as if the Dollar God stands above you with a wad of cash, yet holds it back until you're ready to receive it. It's similar to the saying about learning—"the teacher arrives when the student is ready."

Ben's Experiment

Benjamin was a rep for a company with whom I was consulting. It was a medium-sized distribution company—with 25 sales and marketing reps. Benjamin was the classic under-achiever. You looked at him and could see his talent—but his income and potential weren't in sync. From the first meeting it was obvious he had issues with success. One look at his personal presence, his ward-robe and his lack of passion told me he had some baggage about achievement. Sometimes, people who are in that life-space can actually bring down the rest of the group. I wasn't about to let that happen here. So I pulled him aside after class one day. Here's what the conversa-tion sounded like:

> Don't make friends with people who are comfortable to be with. Make friends who will force you to lever up.
>
> THOMAS WATSON, SR.

Me:	Benjamin, this isn't working is it?
Benjamin:	What do you mean?
Me.	I just feel like we're not getting through to you. Your associates are coming back every week with great success stories and you haven't spoken up once. What's up?
Benjamin:	Bill, the truth is that I've been working here for the past eight years and I do OK. I don't see any way to earn much more than I'm making now. I like your material, but I don't see it making a big difference.
Me:	Ben, here's the problem. Are you ready for it? You're looking at this all wrong. Of course you don't see a way to earn more . . . if you saw a way, you'd be doing it, right?
Benjamin:	I guess so.
Me:	Do you want to try an experiment?
Benjamin:	Sure.
Me:	If you could find a way to double your income from the current level, how much would you be worth, by the hour?

He pulled out his calculator.

Benjamin:	About $100 an hour.
Me:	Answer me honestly now—are you working at that level now?
Benjamin:	No. Probably not.

Then I gave him this exercise:

Me: Go back and look at your planner over the last week. Mark the activities with a red highlighter that you know are not $100 per hour activities. Then I want you to make your plan for next week and have at least five $100 per hour activities in it. Don't ask what they would be. You know intuitively.

The change in him was incredible. How could such a simple exercise have such a huge impact on a person? Over the next four months he went from the middle of the pack to the company's top seller. He went from calling way too low in companies to calling on chief officers. The exercise forced him to challenge how he thought about his earning potential at the company.

The moral is simple. When you connect with what's possible and break it down to daily behavior and attitude, you'll subconsciously find ways to earn even more. Once he saw himself as a $120,000 per year guy, he sought out opportunities that would get him there. For him, the exercise was a way to get ready for success. You, too, should get ready to accept it with grace—because it's deserved. Whatever you want to do, be or have, do some research and begin to get OK with that new future. And presto—before you know it, it falls upon you.

A C T I O N   I T E M

Grab a chocolate chip muffin and a coffee (you'll need some serious caffeine for this one) and come up with the following numbers. This is an exercise to help you re-calculate your per hour rate.

1. How much would you like to earn in the next 12 months? $_____

2. How much time (in "hours per year") do you invest in client/revenue generating activities? _____ Hours/Year

3. Divide #1 by #2. This will give you what your HIGH PRODUCTIVE TIME is worth on a per-hour basis. $_____ /Hour

4. Now, tomorrow ask yourself these questions as you set out to do your task list: **Is this activity worth the hours (#3) I'll invest and will it get me to my goal (#1)?**

Note: Don't calculate "going to kids activities" as part of this. Keep this focused on your "business task list." Recognize that you will always need to do LOW PAY tasks as part of your role.

I merely want you to move into a **new area of consciousness** about your time, your market value and your end result–personal income. As you move into that new consciousness, the market will **automatically** reward your time at a higher rate.

INSIGHT TWENTY-TWO

Things You Shouldn't Say

OLD THINKING	NEW THINKING
Some of my favorite tapes and books have taught me what to say in certain situations.	I must be careful what I say. Words matter.

OK, I fulfilled my promise. I made it through the whole book without telling you what not to say. I can't bear it any longer. There are some things I hear when people call on me that I must address.

I know when I go to a workshop, I am always leery of the guy that stands up front and tells me what to do, what to say and how to think. I say to myself—"if he is so damn good, why is he standing up there making $200 a day doing this?" I know you are probably achieving at a pretty high-level already. I also know you may have been trained to say some of the things below that I'm about to tell you not to say. But my role here is to get you from $50,000 a year to $100,000. Or, from $250,000 to $1,000,000. And it could be that these moves below worked to get you to one level, but will fail to get you to the next level.

Here are the things I want you to take out of your vocabulary—assuming they were there in the first place. The reason I request this is because I speak at a large number of events all over the country. It never fails that after a program some of the participants compliment me on how this material will dramatically change their life and their income. They're happy. We're happy. Another changed life. But then something really odd happens. The same people who complimented us three breaths ago start to babble about their product—and its benefits. Some even begin to solicit our business while we're still next to the podium. They say they have excellent services and prices and they'd love to "earn our business."

Is it possible that the information we imparted just didn't make it through the crust of the tradition? That they've done the old stuff for so long, they cannot depart from it? That's why we've included this chapter—to put it out there right in front of you—what not to say.

"What do I need to do to earn your business?"

Whenever I'm getting sold and someone asks that, I simply say, "You can start by not asking me that. So I guess we're done." This kind of question insults your buyer or prospect at a deep psychological level. It also confirms what the prospect has thought all along—that salespeople are needy and beggars and their only interest in you is as a step to their quota. If you come call on me, please leave this one out of your repertoire.

"I'd like to probe to find out what your needs are."

Probing is done in the medical center or doctor's office, not on a sales call. There are special instruments for probing. No probing—despite what the books tell you. You're not a proctologist. You're a change agent.

"Is that important to you?"

We were taught this in PSS 101 (Professional Selling Skills). I didn't like it then and I still don't. There are two possible outcomes when you ask that question. One—the prospect thinks, "What kind of idiot are you? If it weren't important to me, I wouldn't have just spent fifteen minutes talking about it." Or, he thinks to himself, "Oh, oh. Here he comes—the master salesperson. Sounds like the Fuller Brush man."

As you can see, neither of those outcomes is good for you.

"I'd really like to have a shot at your business."

What is your prospect—a target in the woods? This is a cousin to, "I want to earn your business." To me this says, "I'm not going to ask any questions. I just hope to quote and get lucky." Is this what you really want to look like to your prospect? This goes back to the begging consciousness or the mentality of scarcity. No shooting. No targets. No shots.

"Hello, Marge!" (when you don't know Marge)

I see this when an amateur salesperson comes in off the street. He approaches Marge (her name is on a placard outside her office window) and says, "Hi, Marge, what a beautiful day out there. Is Michael in?" He is practicing what we call "over-rapport." He doesn't know Marge from Adam, but tries to make her feel like she's his long-lost sister. It fails. It always fails. Plus, I love it when she says, "I'm not Marge— she's at lunch."

Remedy

Just be yourself. Don't try to be the person that you don't like calling on you.

A C T I O N   I T E M

Tape yourself—your side of the conversation only. Listen to it and see if you say any of the things in this insight. Even if you don't say them word-for-word—if you even sound like this same person, you will lose ground in selling.

HAVE A UNIVERSAL PROCESS

OLD THINKING	NEW THINKING
Every situation is different. I have to keep changing my approach based on my customer.	I have a process I follow that serves me in any situation in which I find myself. This process is about human nature.

If you're in the business of generating revenue, you are in the business of getting people to make decisions. **You are an agent of change**. The pain most selling companies have is the lack of a strong, simple process that they use in every sales situation. Whether you are a lawyer, a salesperson, or a telemarketer, you need a process to follow. You must also recognize that your prospect goes through a process as they make decisions. The trick is to marry your process with theirs.

In the last 22 insights, we've taken you through some of the concepts we have found make people enormously effective in selling. We've jumped back and forth from the inner game to the outer game and back again.

This insight is about the process from start to finish. We want this to be simple, elegant and profoundly successful for you. The goal of our process is to have it be an elegant journey from inaction to action.

In Neuro Linguistic Programming (NLP), the rule is: *the person with the most flexible system has control of the process.*

As we've built this sales process we've kept that rule clearly in mind. You must be in control of the sales process—not of the people in the process—but of the sales process itself. You decide when it continues, when it is over or when it restarts. You have the ultimate decision, not your prospect. This is a major change in philosophy from

> Let all things be done decently and in order.
>
> *I CORINTHIANS 14:40* KJV

most selling approaches. You run the process. But the process you run is not such a structured sales process that there is no room for movement or flexibility. There is. First, let's review the process and we'll weave in applications as we go. On the next page is a table of the components of your new process (figure 4).

Prelude

The first part of the process is the most important. It deals with how the dialogue begins with your prospect. It deals with conversations between people. It will ultimately determine who gains and maintains control of the sales process.

You've heard the saying, "You only have one chance to make a first impression." That couldn't be more true here—in fact, we'd like to change it to say, "You only have one

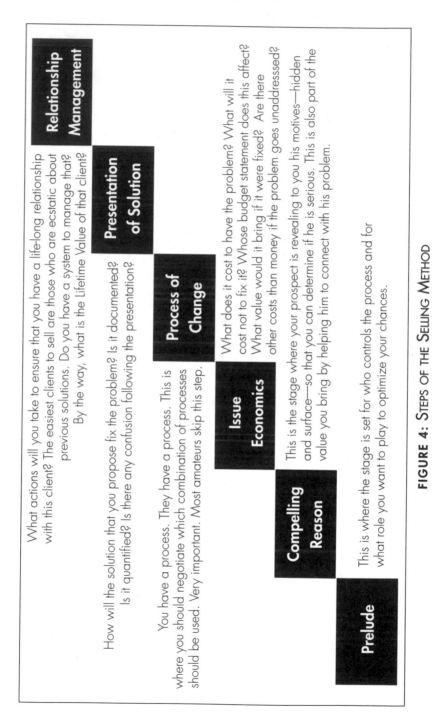

Relationship Management

What actions will you take to ensure that you have a life-long relationship with this client? The easiest clients to sell are those who are ecstatic about previous solutions. Do you have a system to manage that? By the way, what is the Lifetime Value of that client?

Presentation of Solution

How will the solution that you propose fix the problem? Is it documented? Is it quantified? Is there any confusion following the presentation?

Process of Change

You have a process. They have a process. This is where you should negotiate which combination of processes should be used. Very important. Most amateurs skip this step.

Issue Economics

What does it cost to have the problem? What will it cost not to fix it? Whose budget statement does this affect? What value would it bring if it were fixed? Are there other costs than money if the problem goes unaddresssed?

This is the stage where your prospect is revealing to you his motives—hidden and surface—so that you can determine if he is serious. This is also part of the value you bring by helping him to connect with his problem.

Compelling Reason

Prelude

This is where the stage is set for who controls the process and for what role you want to play to optimize your chances.

FIGURE 4: STEPS OF THE SELLING METHOD

chance to begin." The goal is to set the stage for an adult-to-adult relationship where together you discover if there is a fit for an on-going relationship.

The prelude is the tactic you take in the first conversation or meeting with your potential client. We covered it in length in Insight 7. This is where the prospect begins to use his own private logic in answering questions like, "Can I trust this person? Can I like this person? Can I feel safe in inviting this person in? Can I feel comfortable in sharing deep secrets with this person?"

> There are no free moves in sales. Every move has a consequence.
>
> *TERRY SLATTERY*

If he can answer yes to most of those questions, then you have succeeded in your prelude.

The prelude is as much mental as it is physical. You might be saying:

- *I don't know if I can help you, or*
- *I'm not sure what you want to talk about today in our first meeting.*

But you'll be thinking new thoughts like:

- *This person must convince me that he is open to what I am saying, or*
- *This person must convince me that he has a compelling reason to change from his current reality or I will not go forward, and*
- *No one decides whether we go forward but me.*

These are the thoughts that will drive your control of the process. Your thoughts will directly impact the words you say. One important part of the prelude is what we call the up-front agreement. This is a verbal agreement between you and the prospect that determines what should happen in the first meeting.

Here's how it might sound:

> *Mrs. Johnson, I'd like to ask you a few questions about what prompted you to invite me in today. Then you can ask me some questions about my company and how we've helped others. And at the end we can both decide what the next logical step is. Does that sound OK to you?*

By doing this, you are setting the stage for the beginning of a mutually beneficial relationship. If you have to tell him, "Unfortunately, we're not a good fit," at the end, then you've already set it up—up front. You have no worries later on about backing out.

If you think you may have a philosophical conflict with your prospect, this is the time to bring it up. Always talk philosophy, never personality. You could say something like this:

> *Mrs. Jones, you know a little about what we do. I'd like to spend time talking about our philosophy of the kind of person we match up well with and then you can tell me if there is any reason to go further. Does that sound OK?*

------------------------ R U L E ------------------------

*You must not continue with your prospect
to the COMPELLING REASON step until you
first complete the PRELUDE. This is a prerequisite.
Each step is a precursor to the next.*

Compelling Reason

Once you get past the prelude, you must discover what compels the prospect to consider a change. It takes a lot today for people to be open to change, so you must move carefully up front. Just because someone is open to talking to you does not mean they will buy from you—or from anyone. Don't confuse openness with a compelling reason to change. When you discover why your prospect is open to talking with you, you'll also find beneath that openness the compelling and existing condition which will cause him to act or invest.

We addressed two areas of motivation in Insight 9—pain and unexploited opportunities. There are three things you must keep in mind as you begin down this path of discovering what compels your prospect to act.

1. They will not share their deepest pains with you if you don't make it safe to do so. You must keep them safe and non-threatened as they share. The instant you drop into "sell mode" you're finished. So keep your selling self out of it.

> Thinking is the hardest work there is, which is probably the reason so few engage in it.
>
> HENRY FORD

2. Their compelling reasons to be open and buy or solve the problem are never on the surface when you show up. They are beneath the surface. That's why your company pays you a lot of money—to find these buying reasons. It's your responsibility to find the deep pain, not their responsibility to volunteer it. You want the core, revealing, problems—not the shallow information other reps are happy with. The deeper the better.

3. You'll unconsciously let your baggage get in the way of asking the questions necessary to help him discover what those problems are. Your inner voice will start to chirp away at you, "That's none of my business," or "If I ask him that, he'll throw me out of his office." On and on it will chatter. Don't listen to it. Remember that you're unattached. This is part of the process you must go through with him if he's to solve his problem. You owe it to him to

say the things you're scared to say. If you don't, he'll keep hurting.

R U L E

A big part of the value you bring to your potential client lies in the process you take him through. Honor that process and never shortcut it.

R U L E

You must not move forward to the ECONOMICS step until you have completed the COMPELLING REASON step. If you're not convinced he has problems you can fix, then you must walk away. You are in control. Don't weasel out of it. If there is no compelling condition that exists in the prospect's business, then his best conclusion may be no action. And your best decision may be to take it no further. When would you rather discover there is no compelling reason? At the beginning? Or at the end?

Issue Economics

There are three elements to the economics of the decision that directly impact your prospect.

- How much does the problem cost him to have, or how much could the undiscovered opportunity mean to him?
- What's the long-term cost if a decision is made not to fix it?
- What's the prospect willing to budget, both mentally and financially, to get it fixed?

Every decision has a cost to it. If your prospect decides not to fix the problem, then he must know. It's Economic Law # 1—every decision has a price.

Don't think the answers to these questions will come out easily. They won't. You will get resistance from your prospect. Talking about money triggers fear. People are scared to talk about money. Chances are, others (including your competitors) haven't asked him these questions. Questions must be asked in the right way at the right time and in the right place in the process. (See Insight 17).

If the numbers show that the problem is costing him very little, then you can leave the process. It would be foolish to invest $100,000 to solve a $5,000 problem. Recall your intent (from Insight 12)—you are there to help him discover the problem and its impact. Then, after you do that, you can help him fix it.

If you're in a business where there is no loss of money, it doesn't mean there is no cost to the problem. Cost can be in time, hassle, energy, stress, emotion or dollars.

R U L E

Don't move forward until you get a clear understanding of the cost of the problem. If you don't get that from your prospect—or together you can't come up with the cost of doing nothing—then go no further. Find someone else to talk to. Yes, it's a very different philosophy. But, your new quest for achievement demands something different.
Your time is your most precious asset.
Don't waste it on someone who can't say "yes."

Process of Change

If you think that there is only one decision-maker at your prospect company, think again. Seldom is it a single person. The more complex your sale, the more people are typically involved. The way to look at this process is not in the traditional manner of, "Who makes the decision?" If you ask that question, you'll probably get lied to anyway. Plus, they may not even know who makes the ultimate decision—there may be no precedent.

Here's a new way to look at it. You must see the problem they are trying to solve, assuming you have helped them discover it, as the center point of a wheel (see figure 5 below). All the energy must go to understanding and solving that problem. On the inside rung of the wheel, place the people who have the most direct financial impact in solving this problem. These are the people you must get to as you work through the process. You must find their pain, their problem, and their specific spin on the issues before you can go any further.

On the outside ring, list the people who have ancillary impact if the problem either 1) doesn't get solved at all, or 2) doesn't get solved correctly. These are the people who must also be a part of the selling process.

What if you can't get to all these people? Good question. Sometimes you can't. They aren't around. They are in

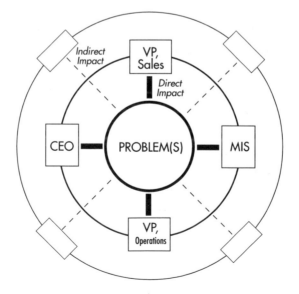

FIGURE 5

remote locations. Or, they just plain won't see you. But the more often you get to these people on both rings, and have conversations with them, the higher your odds will be of solving the entire problem, instead of just one person's corner of the problem.

R U L E

If you aren't comfortable that you've found the compelling reason, the cost of that condition and the process your prospect company will go through, then you cannot move forward. You don't have a real prospect until you've gone through the first four stages.

Presentation of Solution

Here's where you move into the presentation mode. You're helping them see how your product or service will fulfill the needs or pains that they have. There are thousands of books on presentations. But when you read them, be very careful. PowerPoint, while a great media tool, won't make or break your sale. By the time you get to this stage of the

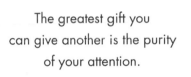

The greatest gift you can give another is the purity of your attention.

RICHARD MOSS, M.D.

process, your future should be well known. If you have carried the process this far, you should be converting 75–90% of your presentations to sales. If you aren't, then you aren't screening hard enough up front.

Another problem that traditional thinking creates for you is the inability of your prospect to pull the trigger and make a decision. This will cost you hours of labor and thousands of dollars in lost opportunity. One way to deal with this is to help them understand clearly what will happen in the event they say "yes" to you. Most salespeople don't even think of this, but we've seen closing rates skyrocket when the next steps after the "yes" are revealed.

Here's what it could sound like. Feel free to change the words to fit your world.

> *Phil, I don't know what the outcome of this presentation will be today but I'd like to give you a snapshot of what the process will look like in the event you want to move forward. First, we'll come out and have a meeting with you and the people who are most impacted by the change, then you and I will get back together for a brief meeting about who to involve in the next step. Then, about a week later, you and I will assemble the team and go over point-by-point the implementation plan. If any problems have arisen by that time, this is when we'll fix them. Does that sound appropriate?*

A master can tell you what he expects of you. A teacher, though, awakens your own expectations.

PATRICIA NEAL

If the above words don't fit exactly in your business, change them to make them work. You must tell the prospect what's going to happen next. You can't blame him if he gets cold feet. Most of us forget that typically we're in front of someone who doesn't buy what we're selling every day of the week. It's up to us to help him.

Relationship Management

Relationship management is not a software package, although software can certainly help you manage your relationships. It's about continuing to solve problems inside your client organization. This is about you becoming a dotted-line provider of solutions to them as a client. Why do most sales organizations spend so much time and money trying to bring in new accounts when all the clients and business they could ever hope to attract are right in front of them? They're blind to it because they do not know how to go back into their current clients and find new problems. They don't think that way. And when salespeople refuse to think that way, they'll waste a lot of precious time trying to sell and acquire new clients when it would be easier to find additional pain in their current clients.

In 1997, Britt Beemer wrote Predatory Marketing (Broadway), a book to bring some straight talk to corporate marketing. As a market researcher, Beemer has done a variety of surveys on the buying habits of American companies. Here's an excerpt that should make the hair on the back of your neck stand up: "Today more than ever, customers are feeling neglected. In a 1997 survey, we found . . . as many as 45% of all business owners state that they are considering buying from another source, other than their number one supplier." Why would that be, you ask? ". . . they feared being vulnerable to the supplier, thereby allowing the supplier to dictate terms to them." I know. I can hear you say, "But we would never do that."

> If most of us are ashamed of shabby clothes and shoddy furniture, let us be more ashamed of shabby ideas and shoddy philosophies.
>
> ALBERT EINSTEIN

You might not, but have you discussed this with your client? Probably not, because that would be a tough conversation to have. But you must have it. There is a one in two chance your client is looking at someone else right now. Make an appointment today and talk about the relationship.

Conclusion

Do you have a relationship management process, which leverages the hard work that you have already done for your clients? If not, get one. Understand how this process fits into your business. Begin by listing all of the problems your product or your company solves and the impact on the customer. If your customer isn't feeling the pain, he won't have a propensity to fix it. One way to start this process is to have what's called a Big Picture Meeting with your client. It is a way to talk about the relationship at a higher level. But don't try to do it in the last five minutes of a normal sales call. It deserves to be done at a higher level, with more people, and with a set agenda. It has to do with the relationship—not on a product or service.

A C T I O N   I T E M

Spend some time thinking about three current deals you're working on and make two lists for each deal. First, list the compelling business condition that will cause them to buy something—and buy from you. If you cannot honestly answer that, then go back and find it.

Second, list the people inside your client company who have the most to gain or lose by a bad decision or no decision at all. If there are people who appear on that list you haven't spoken with about their problems and pain, then call them up and meet with them.

EPILOGUE

Promises

So there you have it. The Caskey Method of selling laid out in 23 insights. So what will happen if you implement these in your business? Good question. Here are three promises I can make.

If you practice these principles you will reach a certainty you've never had before about the sales process. You will be less afraid and more confident as you maneuver through the process. If you don't consider yourself a salesperson, welcome to the growing club of people who understand that you don't have to act like one to be a very good one.

You will reach higher income levels. Let's face it, sales is a place to get your financial needs met. It's also a place you can help others (clients) reach their goals. When your goals match up with theirs, everyone wins. Financially, you should see a 20–100% increase in income over a year's time frame. Over three years of using these insights, you should see 100–500% income growth. If your current compensation plan won't allow you to earn that much, then you have some other answers to find.

Your client wins. Everyone I've talked to who uses this philosophy believes it is in the client's best interest, as well as yours. Honest. Game-free. Straight talk. All of these are words we've heard to describe this method. Be authentic. Be yourself. Just think, riches await you if you will only shed the old selling strategies and adopt a strategy that is closest to the authentic you. People buy from people, not from companies.

Abundance to all.

Cherish your visions; cherish your thoughts; cherish the music that stirs in your heart, the beauty that forms in your mind, the loveliness that drapes your purest thoughts. For out of them will grow all delightful conditions; all heavenly environment of these. If you but remain true to them, your world will at last be built.

James Allen,
As A Man Thinketh

Appendix A
Personal Philosophy

It's OK to read and listen to tapes and consult your mentor, but the end result is up to you. What is your philosophy? What are your rules about achievement? High-income earners know what they will and won't do in the sales process. They are always willing to change something if it doesn't work, but they always have an underlying philosophy of how they work.

In our workshops, we ask people to create their own personal philosophy. It is done to clarify your beliefs about your assets. Below, we've transcribed one of our student's personal philosophies so you can see the extent and depth. Cheryl is a top-income earner at a software company. Read through her notes and see if any of these make sense for you.

1. I will never make a formal presentation to anyone in the prospect-company, unless they have given me three deep, compelling reasons they will buy a system. No less.

2. I will always assess my chances at the end of each call. If I feel those chances drop below 30%, I will call the prospect, decline the invitation to get involved and move on. I am willing to walk at any time.

3. I will never let the prospect get away with unclear statements like "I might do this" or "I think it could

help us." If there is any smoke, I clear it away. My time is too valuable to be dealing with smoke.

4. I believe the most pain in an organization resides in the corner office. I am never afraid to call there, because I know that's where all of the financial pain ends up. If the CEO isn't open to talking about his problems, then I can only assume that he has created that same, closed environment throughout the company. They aren't a prospect.

5. I always talk about money in the first or second call. If I'm not doing that, there is something I'm afraid to bring up. I can't let my prospect down because of my fears and baggage. We don't talk dollars and cents; we talk in round numbers. That keeps them safe.

SIGNED,
CHERYL MASON
V5 SOFTWARE

APPENDIX B
PERSONAL RULES

This is your *Same Game New Rules* Journal. Write down any rules or philosophies you have adopted. You can also use these pages for Action Steps.

RECOMMENDED READING

The following are books, periodicals or monographs that I find particularly useful for people searching for quantum growth in selling achievement. Some are non-conventional and some may be hard to find.

Allen, James. *As a Man Thinketh*. Barnes & Noble Books, 1992.

Buzan, Tony. *The Mind Map Book*. Plume/Penguin, 1993.

Conwell, Russell. *Acres Of Diamonds*. The Berkeley Publishing Group, 1960.

Corkville Briggs, Dorothy. *Celebrate Your Self*. Doubleday, 1986.

Hill, Napoleon. *Think And Grow Rich*. Random House, 1987.

Jarow, Rick. *Creating the Work You Love*. Destiny Books, 1995.

Ponder, Catherine. *Open Your Mind to Prosperity*. DeVorss, 1971.

Rackham, Neal. *Rethinking Your Sales Force*. McGraw-Hill, 1999.

Ray, Michael. *Creativity in Business*. Doubleday, 1989.

Wilde, Stuart. *The Infinite Self*. Hay House Publishing, 1996.

———. *The Trick to Money is Having Some*. Hay House Publishing, 1989.

INDEX

ADVANCED LEARNING SERIES
FROM
CASKEY ACHIEVEMENT STRATEGIES

The Number One Law of Learning is repetition. Because the principles in Same Game New Rules focus on changing thought, they must be reinforced to get the optimum results. Consequently, we have created a list of booklets, books, and audio CDs to help you in your professional growth. Unfortunately, there is no magic pill to learn these principles overnight. They take ongoing study and reinforcement. The Advanced Learning Series has been specially designed to help you make this material intuitive.

Free Online Monthly Newsletter

INCOME INSIGHTS

FREE Report Shows You How To Get the Competitive Edge!

No one has to tell you that in the last 25 years, selling and building a business has changed dramatically. Competition is brutal and ever present, the "final" decision process—the bane of existence for any sales professional—has become so complex, you're simply astounded at how anything is ever accomplished within your prospect's organization.

Not only is time of the essence, but your solution's effectiveness in solving your client's problem is measured not in years, but in weeks or even tomorrow.

The stakes are high! The prospect's final decision will undoubtedly reflect on him and possibly his future within the organization. So what does this obstacle mean to the advanced seller like you?

Simple. You have to be better at what you do!

Most companies concentrate on the "outer game" of their sales force. But to create long term wealth for your business, you or your sales force have to work on your "inner game."

Make no mistake: What you create inside your mind will determine your outer results.

Go to www.samegamenewrules.com to register for newsletter.

Selling from Strength

The Sales Professional's Guide To Growing Your Business And Yourself

Six Audio CD Set and 140 page Operations Manual, includes tips, strategies, interviews, live speeches and more.

For 16 years I've presented over 3000 in-depth seminars (1000 more than Brian Tracy) and have spent 20,000+ hours training professional sale people, business people, and entrepreneurs like you in scores of different industries so they can reach their full potential.

The professionals that I've been privileged to train were not only thrilled with the results of how their personal and professional lives had increased in value...BUT they also realized that when they continually referred back to my training they continued to grow

Like you, I listen closely to my market's needs and respond to it. So I took that extensive training and ruthlessly edited my time tested techniques and strategies into one of the most comprehensive Self-Study Programs on B2B selling that you'll find on the market, today.

For details and audio sample, visit www.SellingfromStrength.com

I invite you to take a journey with me that will deliver you unadulterated success.

   Book/CD set $299.00

Selling From Strength Preview CD

If you think you have a selling process that needs to be improved—if you're intrigued but not sure you're ready to invest $299, then start with the Selling From Strength Preview CD. We've taken two tracks from each of CD's in the kit and combined them onto one preview CD to get you started.

   CD   67 mins $24.95

It's Got to Be Easier Than This

New ideas to change the way you think and feel about business

The path of a professional salesperson is full of frustrations and excitement, obstacles and rewards. We've created this program to help lessen the frustrations, overcome the obstacles, experience more excitement and reap greater rewards. Note that we said HELP. We can't do it for you. It will require some amount of study and contemplation as you go through the audio CD's.

Three Revelations

1. After 3,000 workshops and training thousands of people, I've concluded that the missing link for most organizations is "process." You're the one with the solution to the prospect's problem—so you should have a "process" that guides them from prospect to client to advocate.

2. I believe that most selling models are based on "prospect coercion" and "salesperson fear"—a recipe for mediocre results. Stop the losing game of persuasion and coercion. Start operating from a position of high intent—and watch what happens.

3. My experience with high achievers is that a balanced blend of **spiritual discipline, psychological knowledge,** and **best business practices** yield profound results. **Spirit** is the recognition of your personal value, confidence, and your perspective on the market. **Psychological knowledge** is the study of what motivates people to buy (change). **Best business practices** are the market mechanics that govern how you communicate, who you call on, how you position your value and how you manage the process.

The Bottom Line

Your value deserves to be heard and understood in the world. It's your obligation to develop the skills to express that value effectively.

Two audio CDs, companion workbook and a Personal Power card that will serve as a daily reminder of the Fundamental Shifts necessary in selling.

$69.95

GAINING COMPETITIVE ADVANTAGE

New ideas to make products easier to sell

Over the last 14 years . . . I've worked with quite a few companies helping their sales teams become turbo effective in selling and generating revenue. We do this by CHANGING THOUGHT—CHANGING STRATEGY—and by doing the OPPOSITE of what's traditional.

I see myself as a teacher of **street level execution**—the person who will teach you and your sales teams how to take this message of "Competitive Advantage" and take it to the customers. I went to three clients that we are working with—and selected those in **highly competitive** areas—who use our material and strategies to grow their business and Create Competitive Advantage.

From my research with these three companies came a list of **5 Insights, 3 Rules and 5 Best Practices** of performance.

Here are a few of the things you will learn on this audio.

- Learn how not to fall into the trap of thinking the "competitor" is another vendor.

- If you have any hope of creating a sound competitive strategy, you have to control the sales process—not the people.

- People make buying/changing decisions **emotionally**, so why do you sell **intellectually**? Learn how to impact the emotional aspect of decision-making.

- Learn how to find the pain of the prospect.

- Learn how to get the "no" and move on, instead of just going for the next no.

- Learn how to stop going for the close and create some space where **truth** can happen.

Audio CD $39.95

The Death of Persuasion

The New Sales Model—How To Communicate Your Value

You have been doing business a certain way for decades—communicating and negotiating using the technique of persuasion. And you've been getting decent results. But what if there was a new discovery that could change your paradigm about what motivates customers to buy from you? What if the new paradigm created an entirely new set of standards? What if there were new skills that would have profound impact in how you communicate your value?

Would you want to know about them? We bet you would.

On this CD you will hear about **the new discovery, the new set of standards and the new skills that can profoundly impact your business**. Listen to this CD several times. We're sure you'll be able to relate to this content. You'll learn what we've learned—that most strategies we've been taught about selling and business are antiquated in today's marketplace.

So, are you ready for a new Operating Strategy that could revolutionize the way you communicate and negotiate?

Isn't it time to finally get paid for the value you bring?

Can you afford not to take an hour to listen to this CD?

Audio CD $29.95

Basic Selling Strategies

An introduction to Caskey selling philosophies and methods

Today in the U.S., 200,000,000 people will go to work. Of those, more than 25,000,000 are in positions where part of their responsibility is selling, customer service, or some form of revenue generation. And perhaps you are one of them.

Everyday the situation that you face changes. One day you might be calling on the CEO of a Fortune 500 company. Another day you're trying to hire someone away from one of your competitors. And other days you're trying to hang on to a piece of business that a competitor is pursuing.

Human Nature Never Changes

So with all this chaos, there's usually one thing that never changes—and hasn't for centuries. The work changes because your business changes. But one thing that never changes is **human nature**. You move to and through the marketplace with a lot of value and your role as business professional is to communicate your value so that the marketplace pays you for it.

Best Selling Strategies gives you ongoing, continuous reinforcement of the philosophies we teach. Strategies that have helped thousands of business professionals profoundly redefine their roles in their market and reframe their business relationships so they can achieve higher levels of income and success.

    Audio CD $24.95

49 Tips To Create Wealth In Selling

Portable contemporary philosophy

Selling and building a business is a complex undertaking. Rules have changed in the past twenty-five years. Decision processes are more complex, competition is brutal and ubiquitous, your product advantage is measured in weeks not years, and there is a web of confusion in the buyer's mind about their options.

However, even given those trends, the art of creating revenue is not difficult when you understand some simple and timely concepts: the Inner Game and Outer Game of sales. All of this yields an important truth for advanced sellers—**you will just have to be better at your skills**.

The Outer Game is what is played on the field, the game you play with your buyer or prospect. To create wealth in your business, you need to understand how to play it or you'll be struggling for life—never rising to the income level you deserve.

The Inner Game is the game that goes on inside your head. What you create inside your mind is what determines your "market" results. While some companies work solely on the Outer Game, the most successful companies and their people are working on the Inner environment.

To create wealth in your business and in your personal life, you need to understand how to play the game or you'll be struggling for life, never fully understanding what's happening to you, and never rising to the income level you deserve. What you create inside your mind is what determines your outer results. The most successful companies and their people are working on the inner environment.

Set Booklet & Audio CD - 45 mins $29.95

Design Your Future™

Intensive On-site Training

Who will benefit?

- Sales Teams
- Account Development Teams
- Technical Sellers, (CPA, Engineers, Project Managers)
- Senior Management Teams
- Customer Support Groups

What is it?

Design Your Future™ is a one, two, or three day face-to-face training session, followed by a series of teleconferences. The program is designed to optimize learning through classroom and field time, and reinforcement of material over time.

Why should you care?

Because we cover the issues that are most important to your organization. An example may be to provide professional development that will help the team think differently about the sales process.

How do I know if it's for me?

Design Your Future™ is an ideal program for business-to-business companies with regional, national, or global staff, or for companies that require an immediate high-impact solution.

How will our company be different at the end?

Your staff will:

- Understand the true value they bring to their clients
- Understand "Buyer Behavior"
- Have an effective sales process and know how to control that process

Your company will:

- Generate the right kind and right amount of new business
- See a shorter sales cycle
- Optimize your people asset

What exactly do I get?

Course materials include the Design Your Future™ manual, *Same Game New Rules* book by Bill Caskey, and the Caskey monthly e-newsletter Income Insights. Other materials may be included as deemed appropriate for your group. You also have the option of purchasing audio CD copies of your program.

Call and speak with a Caskey Consultant (877) 639-7853

ORDER FORM

TITLE	ISBN #	MEDIA	PRICE	QTY	TOTAL
49 Tips to Create Wealth in Selling	0-9758510-2-0	Set (Booklet & CD)	$ 29.95	_____	_____
Basic Selling Strategy	0-9722587-6-0	Audio CD (58 mins)	$ 24.95	_____	_____
Gaining Competitive Advantage	0-9722587-3-6	Audio CD (66 mins)	$ 39.95	_____	_____
Income Insights	Nwsltr1	Online	Free		
It's Got to Be Easier Than This	0-9722587-6-0	Book/2 CD set	$ 69.95	_____	_____
Private Telephone Coaching	Coach1	Telephone per hour	$ 500.00	_____	_____
Same Game New Rules—2nd edition	0-9758510-3-9	Book	$ 19.95	_____	_____
Same Game New Rules—2nd edition	0-9758510-4-7	Audio CD (2CDs)	$ 39.95	_____	_____
Selling from Strength	0-9758510-2-8	Book/6 Audio CD Set	$ 299.00	_____	_____
Selling from Strength	0-9758510-8-X	Audio CD (67 mins)	$ 24.95	_____	_____
The Death of Persuasion	0-9758510-7-1	Audio CD (74 mins)	$ 29.95	_____	_____

SubTotal _____

(Indiana residents add 6%) Sales Tax _____

Total _____

Shipping and handling charges $4.00 per order plus $0.95 per item.
All titles ship in 3–5 business days.

Call for quantity discounts 1–877–639–7853 or email info@caskeytraining.com

Name _____

Title _____

Company _____

Address _____

City, State ZIP _____

Phone _____

Email _____

❏ My check is enclosed

❏ Charge my credit card   ❏ Visa   ❏ MC

Card Number_____ Exp Date _____

Signature. _____

FAX TO 317–575–0186

AFTERWORD

Bill Caskey

Bill Caskey has been coaching and developing sales professionals and executives since 1989. His firm, Caskey Achievement Strategies, has worked with thousands of companies in hundreds of industries, including start-up technology companies and more traditional manufacturing companies. To let you in on more of his motives, here is an interview done recently with Mr. Caskey.

Why did you write this?

The first reason is that I had never written anything of length. I thought it would be quite cool to spend the remainder of my life writing, then suffer the same fate as other famous writers—you know, dying an alcoholic, miserable death. So that's #1.

Secondly, and more seriously, I want to have an impact on American business in a grander way than training people one at a time. I wanted to use my experience in the development business by helping today's sales professional re-engineer their thoughts to become profoundly more successful in the market.

Aside from the trends that are effecting business, I wrote this because I saw very weak, almost sad sales approaches and tactics being used by what you and I would consider Top Flight companies. I watched these people and their selling approaches—then I would look at the training they were getting and the books that most of corporate America were reading. It became apparent that we, as a society, aren't teaching much of value to tomorrow's sales forces.

Then, coupled with that observation, I saw people come through our programs, learn our method, learn about psychology, learn about human behavior, learn about themselves and go to the marketplace and blow the lid off of their revenue and income numbers. Plus, they would have no trouble eating the competition for lunch. When I saw that, I realized I had something.

And last, everyday I work with companies who aren't unlike the companies most people work for. There is a lot of pain. Never enough business in the funnel. Too much price pressure. Too much work to advance prospects through the sales process. So I started to come home each night and write about my day and my clients.

Don't a lot of companies already invest in training?

Of course. There's a lot of "training." But is there a lot of learning?

Yes, if you look close enough you will see some companies invest a little in sales training. But the type they invest in is the wrong kind. It's product training. It's feature and benefit training. It's presentation skills. It's industry/trade training. It's team building. All of it is OK stuff, but what they're really doing is acquiring more external knowledge. That's all. They are spending absolutely no time in determining **how** they're going to take that knowledge to the marketplace, have their clients beg for it and get paid for it. They are creating more and more value within the company, but spending almost no development dollars learning how to take that value to a resistant market and get paid handsomely for it.

Plus, they spend very little time dealing with the real issue in sales achievement, and that is the inner landscape of the salesperson. If that inner world is full of garbage and neediness and spiritual barrenness, then what do you suppose the outer world looks like? What do you think that person is going to sound like when he gets in front of a prospect? You got it. He will sound weak. He'll sound self-indulgent. So part of our method is mental, part is physical, but a big part is spiritual—not religious—but spiritual. It has to do with the soul of the seller. The saying is simple: **"You will perform in the marketplace in a manner consistent with your self-image."** How much simpler can you make it? If you want to improve performance, stop working on sales skills, and start working on your self and thinking skills.

There is a myth that if a company hires seasoned veterans, they don't have to invest in training them. Who started that one? I don't find that at all. My best students in this process are 40-55 year-old people who are well-established, good-earners, but who see this group of very aggressive young people coming along and they know they had better work on themselves. I also think there has been a change in our culture, where spending more time on the psychology of self is OK.

When I survey my clients as to what they want to learn more about, it is nearly unanimous—the inner game. I don't think my clients are any more enlightened than the average person. When they are exposed to our philosophies, they realize that is where the action is—the inner self. Once I get inside companies and start talking about these inner concepts, my clients can't get enough of them. "How to think" is the name of the game.

It's almost as if we, as a business culture, have been trained on the surface—but not much deeper. What we are doing is going 1-2-5 levels deeper into the mind of the seller, posing new ways to think about business and sales . . . and then watching turbo growth occur.

Wow! We're on to something here that is vital to the future of our culture. Even the Dali Lama is talking about it—spirituality in business.

What made you think you had the answers when there is so much literature on selling?

Let's get one thing clear up front—I don't have all of the answers. I'm a life-long learner. But my experience with clients has been the best teacher . . . better than any books. We teach expansion of thought. We teach disappearing of the ego. We teach detachment. We teach process management. We teach the attitude of abundance. Nowhere in that list did you hear me talk about probing skills or closing skills or how to make effective presentations. The reason this book is not more of the same is that the same stuff doesn't work. That old stuff is not as important as it was 18 years ago.

I've seen people take their incomes up 200-1000% in a couple of years. Do you think that is really a result of how to probe deeper? No. It's a result of thinking at a deeper level about human dynamics and achievement. It is about having a maturity that allows the individual to say—"OK, I don't have all of the answers. I'm an open book."

I'm a synergist. I didn't create all of this material, although there is a lot that we have alchemized based on sound psychological principles. I am a blender—an alchemist (in a good sense). I take the information that is out there, mix it together, stir it up, add some new elements and serve it. I look at the Internet and books on selling and I see the same old stuff every day. If you want to go to the marketplace and act like everyone else, then read the old stuff. If you want to be treated differently, then read this. Read something new. Learn how to think differently. Who wants to be treated like a used car salesman? Aren't you getting tired of being lied to? I was.

Also, we looked at the sales forces that were coming to us and saw that most of them didn't take their profession seriously. They saw it only as a job. When we asked them why, they told us that the training material that they saw out there didn't apply to their business. What they were really saying is that it didn't apply to them, personally. The material didn't speak to them at a level that caused them to change their approach. There you have it. A bunch of intellectual data, with no soul.

So just because there are millions of info-bytes out there doesn't mean people are reading and learning it. Very little of the data was teaching people how to think differently. I'm not competing against Tom Hopkins, Brian Tracy or anyone else. I'm in a different game.

What was the experience that caused you to get in this business?

Fear. I was always scared throughout life, especially in sales. I had no courage at all. Part of the reason was that I had a messed up inner game. Actually, I spent a part of my life in 12-Step work. Not because it was cool—it wasn't then—but because I was a spiritual wasteland. That's part of me that I'm always working on. That part about "spirituality" being synonymous with "expansion." I had no life philosophy. I had no planned destiny. I had no philosophy of personal expansion. I use a quote early in the book that applies to me—an Arab proverb that says: No man is a good physician who has never been sick.

So I started thinking about processes, thinking methods, and achievement philosophies and came up with the concept of an "**achievement strategy,**" which mixed the outer game and selling philosophies with the inner philosophies of great therapists and philosophers. My goal was to synergize them so that the seller or businessperson had a thinking plan to follow regardless of what situation he or she was in. Overall, I wanted to create a **template of thought** that would apply to everything from interviewing potential employees, coaching your people, and talking with your spouse to, of course, selling and communicating your company's value to your prospective clients. When you think about it, it's all the same. You are in the mode of collaboration to ensure that you each get what you want out of the relationship. Thus, instead of lying, misleading, coercing and convincing, this approach is adult-to-adult and win-win. And because it is a template, it works nearly everywhere.

What would you like to see *Same Game New Rules* do?

For the reader of this book, I would be disappointed if he didn't increase his income by 25% by applying only 3-5 of these insights. It will not take all 23 to improve things. Take something that you do NOT do now that we have addressed within the book and start doing it today. We've even given you action items to try—low-risk things. Practice until you feel like you've got it. We've given you websites, newsletters, additional ways to purchase updates to the information. Try these insights for six months and you should see at least 25% increase in your income. If you're making $100,000 a year, that is the equivalent of $25,000 over the next year. What would you invest to make that happen? Is it worth a few hundred dollars?

As for companies, I hope it does two things: 1) gives them more cash flow, through higher sales and better profits to make their businesses more enjoyable to work in, and 2) helps companies profoundly increase their market value—or net worth. Business is hard today. Consequently, why wouldn't a company take every advantage to grow their market value? Why would there ever be an instant when you would not want to optimize your human resources by developing them with the intent of bringing in even more revenue to the company? Here's another question—why would you ever build a business and not do everything in your power to leverage that business to grow? I can think of no good answers to that.